MARINE ENGINEERIN
Volume 1

GW00788631

Part 9
STEERING GEAR

by

**W. S. PAULIN, B.Sc., C.Eng., M.I.Mech.E.,
F.N.E.C.I.E.S.**

and

**D. J. FOWLER, M.Sc., C.Eng., F.I.Mar.E.,
M.I.Mech.E.**

THE INSTITUTE OF MARINE ENGINEERS

Published for The Institute of Marine Engineers

by

Marine Management (Holdings) Ltd.

76 Mark Lane, London EC3R 7JN

(England Reg. No. 1100685)

Reprinted 1978
Reprinted 1981

Copyright © 1975 Marine Management (Holdings) Ltd.

This book is copyright under the Berne Convention. All rights
reserved. Apart from any fair dealing for the purpose of private
study, research, criticism or review — as permitted under the
Copyright Act 1956 — no part of this publication may be repro-
duced, stored in a retrieval system or transmitted in any form or
by any means, electronic, electrical, chemical, mechanical,
optical photocopying, recording or otherwise, without the prior
permission of the copyright owners. Enquiries should be
addressed to Marine Management (Holdings) Ltd., 76 Mark Lane,
London EC3R 7JN.

ISBN: 0 900976 45 4

Printed by The Chameleon Press Limited, 5–25 Burr Road, London, SW18 4SG, England.

CONTENTS

ACKNOWLEDGEMENTS

The authors and publisher wish to acknowledge the following as sources of illustrations used in this Part and to thank them for their assistance:

Brown Brothers & Co. Ltd.
Donkin & Co. Ltd.
John Hastie & Co. Ltd.
SIG Swiss Industrial Company
Sperry Marine Systems
Kort Propulsion Co. Ltd.
Pleuger Unterwassenpumpen G.m.b.H.
NPL. Ship Division
A. S. Tenfjord MEK Verksted
Porsgrumm Verft A/S and SIG. Swiss Industrial Co.
Svendborg: Motorfabriken Bukh A/S
J. M. Voith G.m.b.H.
Vickers Ltd.
The North East Coast Inst. of Engineers & Shipbuilders

INTRODUCTION

For about 50 years after the introduction of steam propulsion, ships were still being steered by hand. As size and speed increased, the need for power steering led to various devices being tried such as auxiliary steering propellers, swivelling main propellers and jets of water. None of these were found to be practicable and better results were achieved with steam engines or hydraulic rams operating on a rudder. These early mechanisms were started and stopped by hand, the position of the control having no reference to the rudder position.

The problem became acute with the *Great Eastern*—then much the largest ship yet built—as it was found impossible to steer satisfactorily by hand power. In 1867 a steam steering gear fitted with a hunting gear designed by J. McFarlane Gray—a founder member of the Institute of Marine Engineers—was installed on the *Great Eastern*. For the first time this gave power steering which could be controlled by a steering wheel, operated in a similar manner to hand steering gear, but with no "kick-back" on the handwheel.

For many years steering gears were placed on or near the bridge. This was because the handwheel movement was transmitted to the engine control through shafting and bevel wheels and there was a practical limit to the distance through which this method of transmission was effective. The steering engine actuated the rudder by means of rods and chains, extending along the deck from the chain barrels of the engine to the quadrant or tiller keyed to the rudder stock. Failure of these gears, particularly in the rod and chain transmission, was at one time fairly common and this finally led in 1936 to the appointment by the Board of Trade of a Committee of Inquiry into Steering Gears. The findings of this Committee drew attention to a number of deficiencies in the design, operation, maintenance and inspection of steering gears. This led to the adoption of higher standards and hence to the safer operation of ships generally.

In 1888 however, A. Betts Brown patented a hydraulic telemotor which provided the facility of an easy remote control and this led to the evolution of machines such as Wilson–Pirrie, Brown Steam Tiller and hydraulic steering gears which could act directly on to the rudder stock.

Until 1911, the power to operate steering gears was always basically steam, since even hydraulic steering gears were activated by water pressure from a hydraulic mains system which also served other auxiliaries such as derricks, hoists etc., the system being powered by a steam pump.

In 1911 however, the first motor ships were built and since steam was not available, electrical power had to be used. The availability of variable stroke reversible pumps, in the form of the Hele–Shaw and Williams–Janney designs, enabled these pumps to be used in association with continuous running electric motors for the purpose of providing hydraulic power for the operation of steering gears. The control of the steering gear movement was achieved entirely through the medium of the stroke of the pumps. This combination has proved to be eminently suitable for the purpose and is still very much in favour.

About the time of the introduction of the electrically driven hydraulic steering gear, direct electric steering gears were also introduced. These consisted of stopping, starting and reversing motors mechanically coupled to the rudder head, the control from the bridge being electrical.

The special need for smaller ships such as trawlers, tugs and coasters to have both hand and power steering from the bridge was satisfied for many years by a combined hand and steam or electrical chain gear being placed on the bridge. About 1930, hand and power hydraulic gears were introduced in which a rotary hand pump on the bridge could be used to control power steering, or provide direct hand steering by being connected to the main cylinders.

A combined rudder carrier and vane type hydraulic rudder brake was patented by McGregor in 1935. The rudder brake was a very desirable fitting in the case of chain steering gears since in the event of a failure in the transmission, the rudder could be quickly brought under control. A further advantage was that the vane brake could be converted into emergency steering gear by use of a hand pump. This method of controlling the rudder stock was later developed into the present day rotary vane gear.

The fitting of an automatic helmsman became increasingly popular between the wars and these units are now almost universally fitted on ocean going ships, either as an alternative to manual control by means of a hydraulic telemotor or as the only controlling unit. In this latter case the emergency non-follow up switch for manual control with which automatic helmsman units are provided is regarded as the alternative control from the bridge and the electrical system associated with this manual control is separate and additional to the system for the main control.

1. SOME STEERING GEAR RULES AND DESIGN CONSIDERATIONS

1.1. RULES

The vital importance of steering gears to the safety of ships need not be emphasized but is clearly the reason for the wide degree of control which is exercised over their design and performance. Some of the more important Rule requirements are given below, but for fuller information on this subject reference should be made to the relevant Government Regulations and to the Rules of the Classification Societies. The Rules which follow are not taken solely from those of any Authority but are recorded here as being of most interest to the reader, who should be aware that some variations do exist in the Rules of the different authorities. Account has also been taken of some proposed amendments to the convention of Safety of Life at Sea (SOLAS) Regulations which are likely to take effect in the near future. Those concerned with meeting the requirements of any particular Authority are cautioned therefore to refer directly to the Rules of the Authority concerned.

1.1.1. Main and Auxiliary Steering Gear

All ships must be provided with an efficient main and auxiliary steering gear and except for very small vessels the main steering gear must be power operated. The auxiliary steering gear must also be power operated when the Rule diameter of the rudder stock exceeds 230 mm for passenger vessels and 250 mm for cargo vessels, although the lower figure of 230 mm is likely to apply to all vessels in a few years time.

Whilst it is desirable that the main and auxiliary steering gears should be entirely independent of each other, this is rarely achieved in practice since both gears commonly share a hydraulic actuator which may or may not be duplicated.

The main steering gear, with the ship at her deepest seagoing draught, must be capable of putting the rudder over from an angle of 35° on one side to 35° on the other side with the ship running ahead at maximum service speed. It must also be capable of putting the rudder over from 35° on either side to 30° on the other side in not more than 28 sec, under the same conditions.

The auxiliary steering gear need only be capable of steering the ship at navigable speed but it must be capable of being brought speedily into action

3

in an emergency. Navigable speed is generally considered as one half of the maximum service speed ahead or 7 knots, whichever is the greater.

Where the main steering gear comprises two or more identical power units, an auxiliary steering gear need not be fitted in a passenger vessel provided that with one unit out of action the gear is capable of putting the rudder over in 28 sec in the manner above. A similar ruling applies for cargo vessels but with the less onerous condition that the steering gear need only meet the above requirement for auxiliary gear, with all power units operating simultaneously.

For the above to apply, it is essential so far as is reasonable and practicable, that a single failure in the main steering gear power units or piping will not impair the integrity of the remaining part of the steering gear.

The steering gears, both main and auxiliary, are required to be of adequate strength for their respective duties as already defined. The main steering gear must also be designed so as to ensure that at maximum astern speed neither the gear nor the rudder stock will sustain damage.

1.1.2. Rudders

In passenger ships where the Rule diameter of the rudder stock exceeds 230 mm, an alternative steering position remote from the main position is to be provided and must be arranged so that failure of either system cannot render the other system inoperable. Provision must be made to transmit orders from the bridge to the alternative position.

The exact position of the rudder, if power operated, must be indicated at the main steering position and the method of indication must be independent of the steering gear control system.

An efficient locking or brake arrangement must be fitted to all steering gears to enable the rudder to be maintained stationary if necessary.

All power operated gears must be fitted with arrangements for relieving shock. This is a requirement to protect against the action of heavy seas against the rudder. The relief valve provided with some fixed displacement pumps operating hydraulic steering gears. Para. 2.6 do not afford protection against such shocks on the main actuators thus relief valves as described in Para 6.9.1 must also be provided.

Suitable stopping arrangements are to be provided for the rudder so as to restrict the total travel. Cut outs on the steering gear are to be arranged to operate at a smaller angle of helm than those for the rudder.

1.1.3. Electrical Supply

The more important provisions for electric and electro hydraulic steering gears are as summarized below. Only short circuit protection and overload alarm are to be provided in steering gear circuits.

Indicators for running indication of steering gear motors are to be installed on the navigation bridge and at a suitable machinery control position.

Each electric or electro–hydraulic steering gear consisting of one or more power units shall be served by at least two circuits fed from the main switchboard. One of the circuits may pass through the emergency switchboard. Each circuit is to have adequate capacity for supplying all the motors which are normally connected to it and which operate simultaneously. Similarly, if transfer arrangements are fitted in the steering gear room to permit either circuit to supply any motor or combination of motors, the capacity of each circuit is to be adequate for the most severe load conditions. The circuits must be separated throughout their length as widely as practicable.

On smaller vessels, if the auxiliary steering gear is powered by a motor primarily intended for other services, alternative protection arrangements to those described might well be acceptable.

Where electrical control of the steering system is fitted, an alternative system is to be installed. This may be a duplicate electrical control system or control by other means.

1.2. SPECIAL REQUIREMENTS

Owners may specify additional requirements such as faster hardover to hardover time, strength above that required by the Rules, additional control points and additional duplication.

1.3. RUDDER TORQUE

Formulae for assessing rudder torques are based upon the expression

$$T \propto A C_p V^2 \sin \theta$$

where T = rudder torque

A = rudder area

C_p = centre of pressure distance from centre line of rudder stock

V = velocity of ship

θ = rudder angle measured from mid-ship position.

In practice, different constants obtained empirically are used with this expression and take into account such factors as propeller slip and wake speed as appropriate, depending upon the location of the rudder in relation to the propeller.

The position of the centre of pressure can have a significant effect upon rudder torque and, hence, on the size of a steering gear. In simple "barn door" type rudders of single screw vessels, no adjustment can be made; but

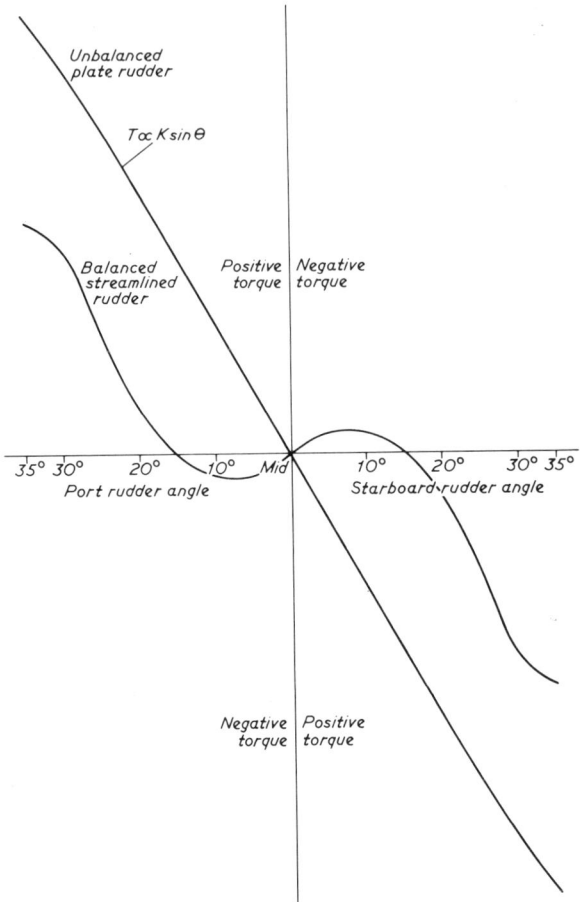

FIG. 1.—*Typical torque characteristics for a spade type balanced rudder.*

in fully balanced rudders of the spade type, such as are often fitted to twin screw ferries, the position can be adjusted by the designer to give the optimum position. This lies between 30 and 32 per cent abaft the leading edge of the mean chord of the rudder. Such a rudder would have its centre of pressure forward of the stock position at low helm angles, would balance around 10° to 15° and drift aft of the stock at higher rudder angles.

This assures easy handling by the helmsman in small vessels where a hand operated gear is fitted, as the rudder would have the tendency to move out towards the balancing point, while at higher angles it would tend to return to midships. Figure 1 shows a typical torque characteristic for a spade type balanced rudder, which has the advantage of reduced maximum torque demand at hardover and of very low torque demands at low rudder angles.

The astern torque should also be calculated. As with some rudder designs, notably balanced rudders, this torque can be higher than the ahead torque. It is normal to calculate astern torques on the basis of astern speed being half of the ahead speed unless even higher astern speeds have been specified in the design.

1.4. HORSEPOWER

The peak horsepower that a steering gear must develop is the product of the maximum torque (T), usually at hard over with the ship travelling at full speed, and the maximum speed (S) of rudder movement, i.e.

$$\text{Horsepower (max)} \propto T \times S.$$

The combination of maximum torque and speed can only exist for some two or three seconds during each such manoeuvre; so clearly, the average-power required to operate the steering gear is considerably below the peak. Because the steering gear must have sufficient power to overcome friction and still have ample reserve of power, the value for T used in the above horsepower expression is significantly higher than that used in the expression for rudder torque.

When considering the diameter of the rudder stock above the main bush account must also be taken of bending stresses introduced by steering gears in addition to the shear stresses generated by the steering gear torques. With rotary vane and four ram twin tiller gears with all cylinders in operation, there are no bending stresses introduced, but with other actuators bending forces are present and must be taken into account.

Bending stresses created by the rudder hydrodynamic forces are normally restricted by the design to that part of the rudder stock below the main bush. However, if wear in the rudder stock main bush is allowed to become excessive with spade rudder designs of the overhung type, then bending stresses of a dangerously high order can frequently be transmitted up the rudder stock and above the main bush—so as to cause failure in the vicinity of the steering gear connexions.

2. CONTROLS

2.1. STEERING GEAR ASSEMBLY

A typical steering gear assembly illustrated by the block diagram in Fig. 2(a) consists of a steering wheel on the bridge operated by the helmsman from which the "helm applied" order is transmitted to the steering engine control. The resultant actuation of this control causes the steering engine to move and with it the rudder to which it is connected.

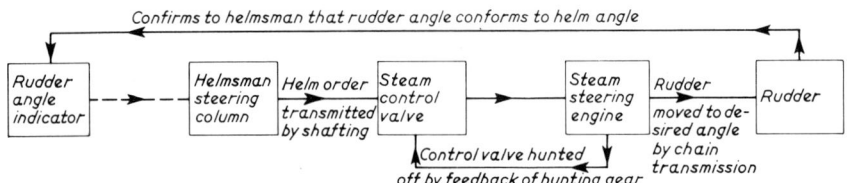

(a)—*Steam steering gear with shafting control and chain drive.*

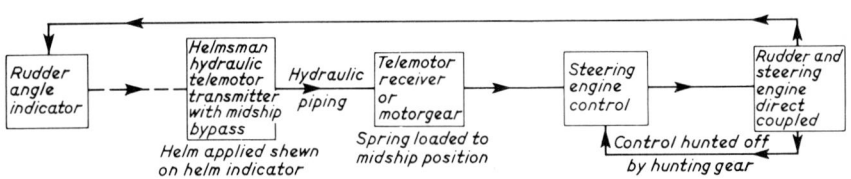

(b)—*Hydraulic telemotor with midship bypass controlling steering gear with hunting gear.*

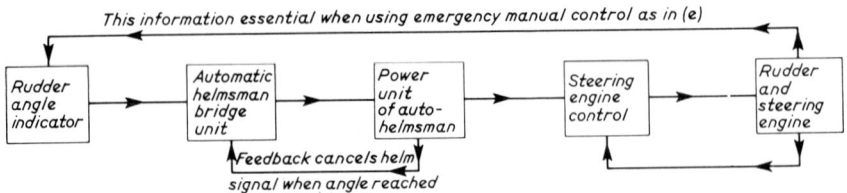

(c)—*Automatic helmsman controlling steering gear with hunting gear (can be combined with telemotors (b) and (c) above in bridge console in Fig. 6).*

8

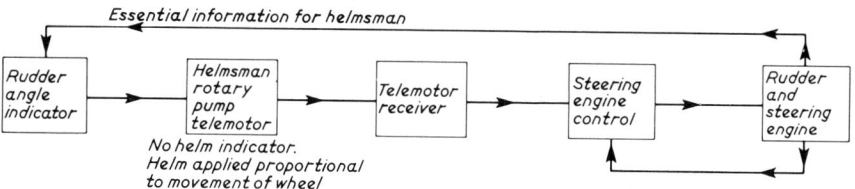

(d)—*Rotary pump telemotor controlling steering gear with hunting gear.*

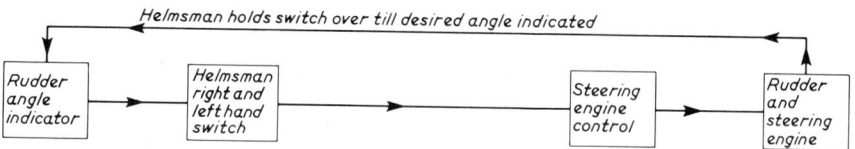

(e)—*Non-follow up steering gear, i.e. no hunting gear (also shows control circuit of emergency manual control on automatic helmsman).*

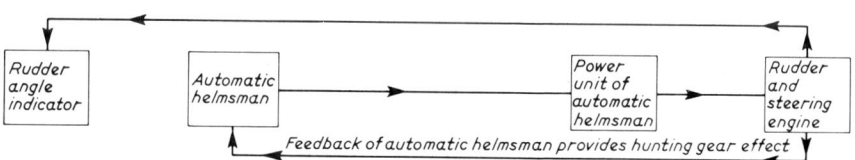

(f)—*Automatic helmsman controlling non-follow up type steering gear (complete unit incorporates combination in (e) as alternative control).*

FIG. 2.—*Block diagrams of typical combinations of steering gear control systems.*

Information that the "helm applied" order has been obeyed is fed back automatically through "hunting gear" to the steering engine control, causing it to cut off power to the steering engine so that it will stop when the desired rudder angle has been reached. (Sections 4.2.1, 6.1 and 6.7.1.)

Helm angle is the position of the steering wheel relative to midships. As will be seen from the descriptions which follow, the steering wheels of some control systems maintain a fixed relationship with the rudder. In such cases an indicator pointer geared to the handwheel registers the helm angle, informing the helmsman of the angle the rudder will take up, assuming that the units making up the steering gear assembly function correctly. Unfortunately, as this does not invariably occur, the Rules now require that an independent rudder angle indicator is fitted when the rudder is power operated. (Section 1.1.2).

In other steering gear systems, the steering wheel does not maintain a fixed relationship with the rudder so that a helm indicator geared to the steering wheel cannot be provided, and hence the independent rudder indicator is essential. The different types of control commonly in use are described hereunder.

2.2. Shafting Control

This method of connecting the steering wheel (Fig. 2(a)) so as to operate the steering engine control was extensively used in conjunction with steam steering gear driving the rudder by means of rods and chains. Because of the direct connexion of the bridge handwheel to the steering gear control, true indication of the helm position is given by a pointer on the steering column geared to the handwheel. This method is not suitable for remote control.

2.3. Hydraulic Telemotor with Midships Bypass

Hydraulic telemotors were evolved in order to provide the remote control for which shafting drive had proved unsatisfactory. Figure 2(b) shows a typical application. A transmitter on the bridge operated by the steering wheel is connected by piping to a receiver, sometimes called "motorgear", coupled to the steering engine control. As will be seen from the descriptions which follow, elaborate devices ensure that the receiver moves with the transmitter and keeps in step with it, so that the handwheel will maintain a fixed relationship with the receiver. This enables a pointer geared to the handwheel to indicate the helm angle to the helmsman.

2.3.1. Donkin Bridge Transmitter

Figures 3, 4 and 5 illustrate three forms of bridge transmitter. The transmitter illustrated in Fig. 3 has two cylinders which are connected by copper pipes to two receiver cylinders at the steering engine. Plungers work in the bridge transmitter cylinders operated by racks which engage the opposite sides of a pinion which is connected by gearing to the handwheel. Thus, when the handwheel is turned so that ram (A) rises and the other ram (B) falls, liquid is forced along one pipe and returned along the other. The cylinders of the motor gear or receiver in the steering gear compartments are in line and back to back, the rams being connected by links. The liquid from the transmitter forces ram (C) out pulling ram (D) into its cylinder, which transfers an equal volume of fluid back to the transmitter.

The receiver rams are loaded by springs (E) towards midships, and valves (F) and (G) in the transmitter are opened by cam (H) when the handwheel is midships, bypassing the transmitter cylinders by opening the two sides of the system to each other. This allows spring (E) to push the receiver to midships if it is not there already. Simultaneously, the bypass valves expose the hydraulic system to suction valve (J) and relief valve (K) in the make up tank, allowing replenishment liquid to be sucked in or surplus liquid to be blown off if necessary.

Thus, the bypass valves allow the system to balance itself and adjust its liquid charge automatically every time the handwheel is midships. When the handwheel is turned from midships, the bypass valves close and the two sides of the system are separate.

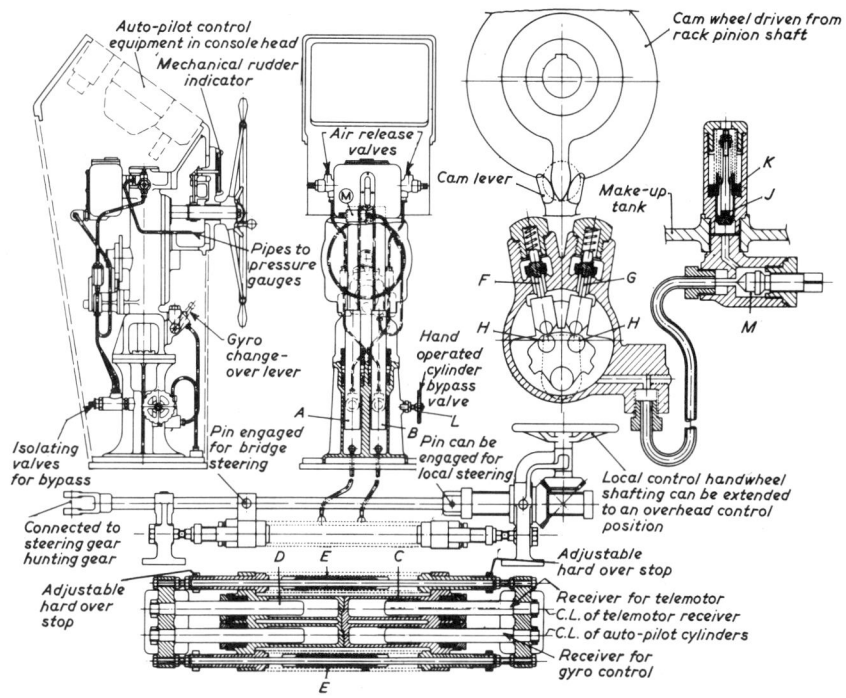

FIG. 3.—*Donkin duplex ram hydraulic bypass telemotor.*

2.3.2. Hastie Bridge Transmitter

The telemotor in Fig. 4 also has a ram type transmitter and automatic mechanically operated bypass valves, but a very desirable feature of maintaining a pressure in the system is achieved in a different way which is described in Section 2.3.5 below.

2.3.3. Brown Bridge Transmitter

Figure 5 shows a telemotor with a similar motor gear to the one already described, but the bridge transmitter consists of a piston in a single cylinder which is reciprocated by a rack geared to the handwheel. Bypassing at midships is effected by means of ports in the cylinder arranged so that when the piston is in the midship position, the ports which are immediately above and below the piston communicate with a common chamber. This, in turn, is connected to the make-up tank, thus providing the same bypassing characteristics and liquid adjustment facilities described for the previous telemotors.

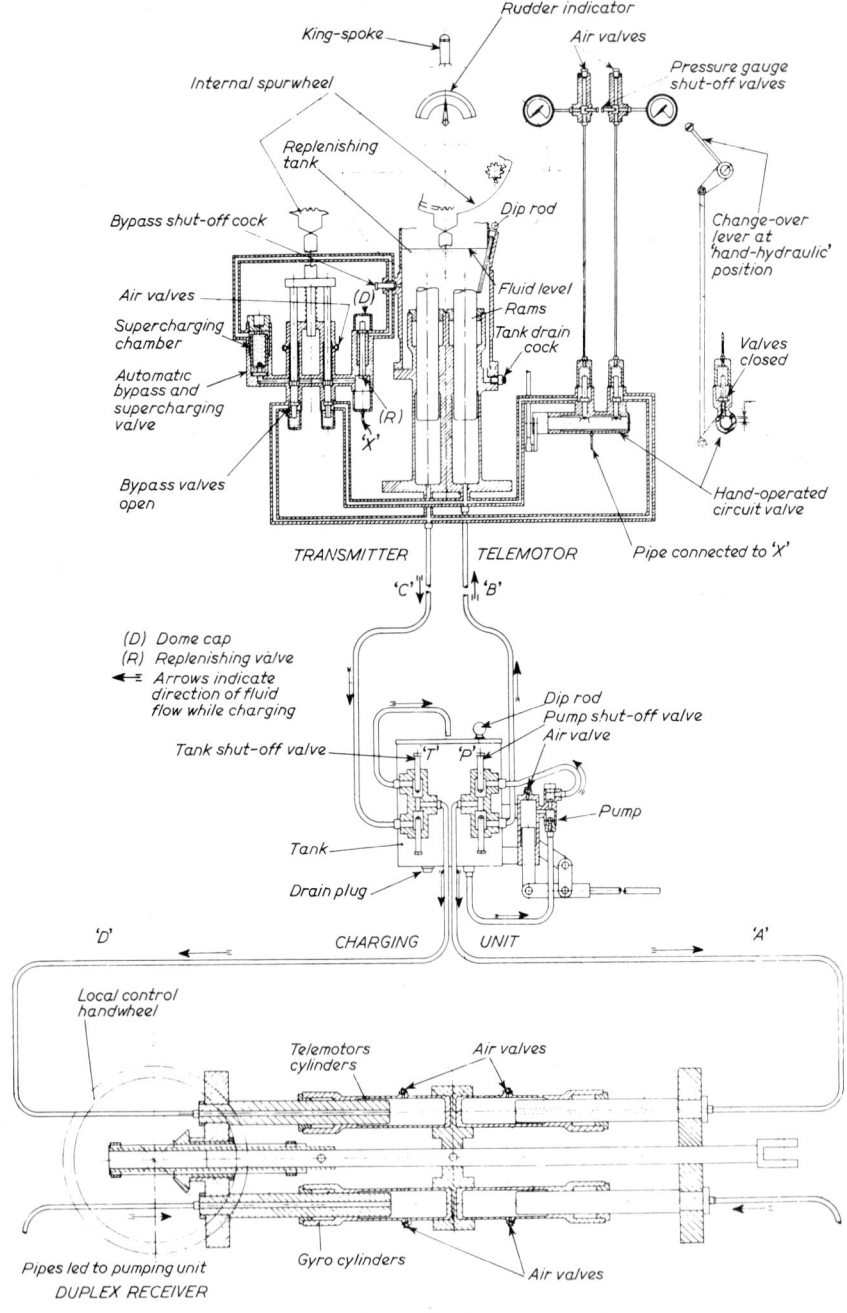

FIG. 4.—*Charging diagram for Hastie bypass telemotor.*

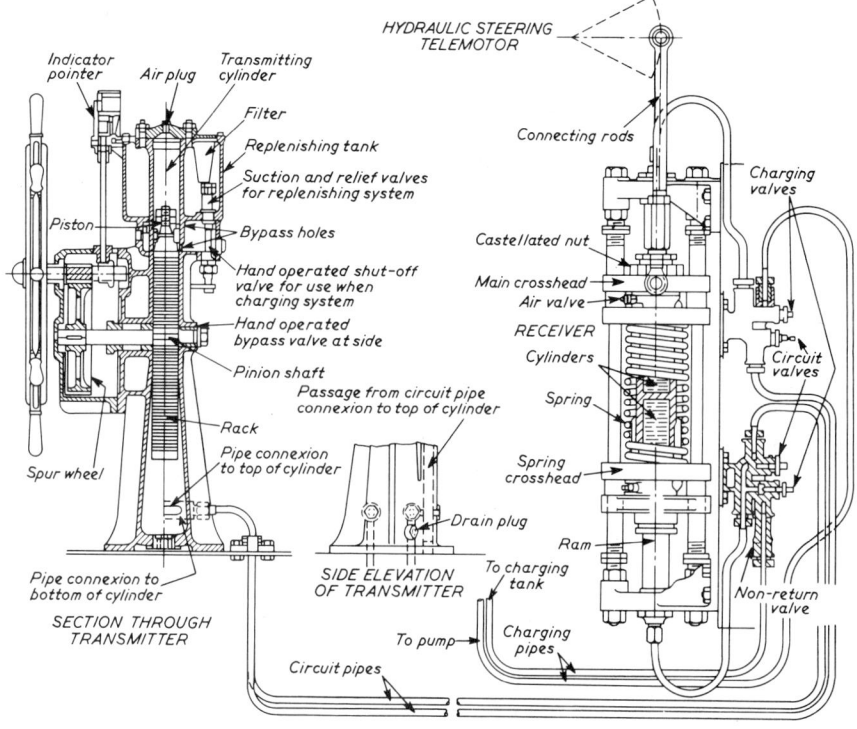

FIG. 5.—*Brown Bros. bypass piston telemotor.*

2.3.4. MacTaggart Bridge Transmitter

Another well known make, the MacTaggart telemotor, has hand operated bypass valves. A lever at the side of the column can be lifted to open the bypass valves at midships, a cam prevents lift in any other position.

If the helmsman feels slackness or overtightness of the handwheel, or lack of balance at midships indicated by unequal readings of the pressure gauges, he lifts the hand bypass lever. By communicating the system to the suction and relief valves in the make-up tank and bypassing the transmitter cylinders, the same corrections occur as have been described as the result of the opening of automatic bypass valves.

2.3.5. Bypass Telemotors—General

It is an advantage for a telemotor to have a slight initial pressure as this ensures immediate response to helm changes. The telemotor shown in Fig. 3 is so arranged that when moving from the midship position, the valve on the pressure side closes immediately, before the valve on the other side closes. This means that this side is still open to the make up tank, and because the ram is being pulled out of the cylinder, a slight negative pressure is created which causes the suction valve in the make-up tank to open and admit a small extra amount of fluid into the system. The valve then closes and the effect now is that the whole system is slightly supercharged. The relief valve in the make up tank is set at 5·5 bar (80 lb/in²), thus maintaining this initial pressure. A similar effect is produced in the telemotor shown in Fig. 5. When the piston on the pressure side moves to close the bypass port, simultaneously it leaves the other side of the system open to the make up tank through the bypass port enabling extra fluid to be sucked in.

The bypass valves of the telemotor illustrated in Fig. 4 open and close simultaneously, so a special supercharging unit is provided which is located between the replenishment tanks and the bypass valves and is fitted with a load replacement piston. Each time the transmitter approaches the midship position, the tappet rods enter, generating pressure in the supercharging chamber and causing the displacement piston to lift against its spring. The piston loading is such that when raised it exerts the required fluid pressure in the chamber.

Normally provision is made with these telemotor systems to enable manual handwheel control of the steering units to be carried out at the steering gear itself. For this purpose a locking pin arrangement, as shown in Fig. 3, is provided so that the steering gear control can be isolated from the receiver and connected instead to the handwheel so that local operation of the gear can be carried out.

Telemotor receivers have adjustable stops which are set to operate at the hard over positions, just before similar stops on the steering gear come into action. This ensures that pressure on the handwheel at hard over when no further movement is possible, will not cause undue strain on the valve mechanism of the steering gear.

These telemotors can all be fitted into bridge consoles, which also house automatic helmsmen (Fig. 6.) When used with an automatic helmsman, a lever with "Hand" and "Gyro" positions is mounted on the column inter-locked with a switch.

In the "Hand" position, the hydraulic telemotor is in control and the automatic helmsman is switched off.

In the "Gyro" position, the automatic helmsman is in control, and the hydraulic telemotor is bypassed which permits its receiver, which is still coupled to the steering engine control, to move about freely without inter-fering with gyro control.

When a steering wheel control is moved quickly to actuate the rudder, it will cause the steering engine control to move to the fully open position. Once this condition has been reached the maximum rate of movement of the rudder is obtained and further movement of the handwheel can no longer increase the rate of movement of the rudder. It may, however, result in damage to the steering control mechanism if undue force is exerted by

FIG. 6.—*Combined bridge console incorporating hydraulic telemotor and automatic helmsman. Top raised to show automatic helmsman; hydraulic telemotor is housed in lower part of column.*

the operator in a mistaken effort to achieve faster movement of the rudder.

Telemotor operating pressures vary with different makes, but normal working maximum pressures fall within the range 28–41 bar (400 to 600 lb/in²). Occasionally, gressures as high as 55 bar (800 lb/in²) may be necessary, but no normal conditions should need as much as 69 bar (1000 lb/in²).

2.3.6. Charging Fluid

The correct charging fluid must be used in a telemotor. This may be either a fifty–fifty mixture of glycerine and water, or "Kilfrost" and water which have freezing points of −23°C (−9°F) and −29°C (−20°F), respectively; Alternatively, one of the special telemotor oils can be used which have pour points of the order of −40°C (−40°F) and viscosity at 21°C (70°F) from 90 to 130 sec Redwood 1. The oil used for charging a steering gear is not suitable, as even such oils with low pour points are too viscous for this type of telemotor and would make the wheel very heavy to operate.

2.3.7. Charging

It is not possible to give detailed charging instructions for each make, however the following procedure applies in general to all telemotors with midship bypass:

 a) Disconnect receiver by transferring change over pin to local control.
 b) Blow through pipe leads with compressed air then wash out with water if charging fluid "Kilfrost" or glycerine and water solution or with paraffin if telemotor oil.
 c) Operate valves and insert circuit pipes if required as recommended by makers.
 d) Pour fluid into charging pump tank through filter provided. Maintain level in this tank throughout operation.
 e) Pump round with charging pump. Fluid will return to charging tank in steady stream changing to spurts in time with pump strokes as air expelled.
 f) Operate valves to normal working positions leaving slight pressure on system before shutting off charging pump.
 g) Turn steering wheel side to side blowing air off at cocks on transmitter and receiver cylinders. System should build up to initial pressure approximately 5·5 bar (80 lb/in²).

2.3.8. Checks

The handwheel should tend to spring back when moved approximately two spokes either side of midships, indicating that receiver has moved to compress return springs.

 1) Take wheel hardover till receiver against stops.
 2) Chock handwheel.
 3) Receiver should hold against stop for half an hour.

4) Repeat other side.
5) Insert pin connecting receiver to engine control.
6) Check that direction of rudder movement is correct.
7) Check that hardover stops on receiver bear equally and operate before stops on steering engine.

Causes and remedies relating to bypass type hydraulic telemotors are given in Table I.

2.4. Pump Type Telemotors

The essential difference between the transmitters of telemotors with midships bypass and pump type telemotors is that the travel of the bypass type transmitter from midships is limited by the ram or piston butting the cylinder end, whereas the rotary pump operated by the handwheel on a pump type transmitter can be turned indefinitely in either direction and it has no fixed midship position.

This characteristic makes it suitable for the purpose for which it was originally designed, namely to operate steering gears providing hand and power steering from the bridge. The handwheel driven pump can be used to control power steering with relatively few turns from hardover to hardover, and also to carry out hand steering with many more turns from hardover to hardover—the actual number varying with the rudder torque which decides the capacity of the rudder actuator.

2.4.1. Application

Figure 2d shows a typical pump type telemotor application which provides for power steering from the bridge. A typical bridge unit is shown in Fig. 7.

A make up tank in the top of the steering column is connected to the pump via a shuttle valve, which when the handwheel is turned, automatically closes on the pressure side, simultaneously opening the suction side to the tank. This ensures that the system will keep fully charged provided the oil level of the make up tank is maintained, and air can readily escape as one side of the system is always open to the make up tank.

The pump in Fig. 7 is a fixed tilt swashplate pump of precision manufacture capable of holding the operating pressure with very little leakage. The fact that leakage does occur, however, means that while movements of the receiver are proportional to movements of the handwheel, it is not possible to maintain the exact relationship inherent in the ram type telemotor with midship bypass.

This means that it is not possible to indicate the helm angle by means of a pointer geared to the handwheel. Thus, the helmsman, while he knows that the change of rudder angle will be proportional to the amount of movement he gives to the handwheel, he has to rely on the rudder indicator to be informed of the exact angle to which he has moved the rudder.

TABLE I—FAULTS, CAUSES AND REMEDIES IN BYPASS TYPE HYDRAULIC TELEMOTORS*

Fault	Cause	Remedy
1. Make up tank requires frequent topping up.	External leaks.	Examine joints and ram glands for leaks. Tighten or remake joints. Renew packing if necessary. If rams scored or worn hollow 0·20 mm (0·008 in) or more. Renew.
2. Rudder will not hold helm angle away from midships. Slips back towards midships.	a) External leaks.	Procedure as above.
	(b Internal leaks.	Make sure hand bypass valve properly closed. Check whether automatic bypass valves leaking by closing bypass isolating valves and holding wheel over. If creep stops, leave isolating valves closed, close valve to shut off makeup tank. Examine bypass valves while continuing steering. If telemotor with piston type transmitter examine leather packing and cylinder for scores or wear. Renew.
3. Wheel slack no initial pressure. Excess movement before receiver moves.	Air in system.	Make sure make up tank level has been maintained and that tank and bypass isolating valves are open. Blow air off transmitter and receiver cylinders. Move wheel smartly side to side of midships. Initial pressure should build up. If not, check that suction valve is not sticking. If excess air in system pump round until return spurts solid with pump strokes. See "Charging", para. 2.3.7.
4. Excess movement before receiver moves but initial pressure satisfactory.	Excess midship bypass opening.	Valves open too long due to excessive lift. If piston type transmitter, piston leathers too shallow allowing excess port opening. Adjust.
5. Receiver does not return to midships when transmitter at midships.	a) Bypass not functioning.	Open hand bypass. If receiver then returns to midships bypass not working due to no lift at midships. If piston type transmitter, piston leathers too deep, covering bypass ports. Adjust.

6. Wheel stiff.	b) Broken receiver return spring.	Examine and renew if necessary.
	c) Seizure in receiver or steering engine hunting gear.	Disconnect receiver from engine to isolate fault. Free and lubricate.
	a) Excess initial pressure in system.	Check that relief valve in make up tank is free and correctly adjusted. Should relieve at 5·5 bar (80 lb/in²) on external bypass valve telemotors and at 17 bar (250 lb/in²) on piston type transmitter telemotors.
	b) Mechanical binding in receiver or hunting gear.	Disconnect receiver from engine control if then free, fault is in engine control; examine, free and lubricate hunting gear. If receiver stiff, clean and grease rams if charging fluid is Kilfrost or glycerine and water. If rams grunt with oil charge, renew packing.
7. Steering wheel takes charge and runs hardover.	Severe seizure in steering engine control which holds control in open position and prevents it hunting off.	Action of hunting gear is to drive telemotor receiver which pumps fluid into transmitter, driving hand wheel. Locate seizure and clear.
8. Engine, tiller, rudder and rudder indicator not simultaneously midships.	a) Rudder indicator incorrectly adjusted.	Check reading with tiller midships. Adjust if necessary.
	b) Receiver links require adjustment.	Adjust if receiver at midships and engine not at midships.
	c) Receiver and engine midships, quadrant not at midships.	Engine pinion incorrectly engaged in quadrant teeth.
	d) Tiller midships, rudder not midships.	Rudder stock twisted. Adjust so that rudder at midships when helm at midships, temporarily, until repairs can be effected.

* It is not possible to give precise instructions for individual makes. The table should be regarded as a general guide.

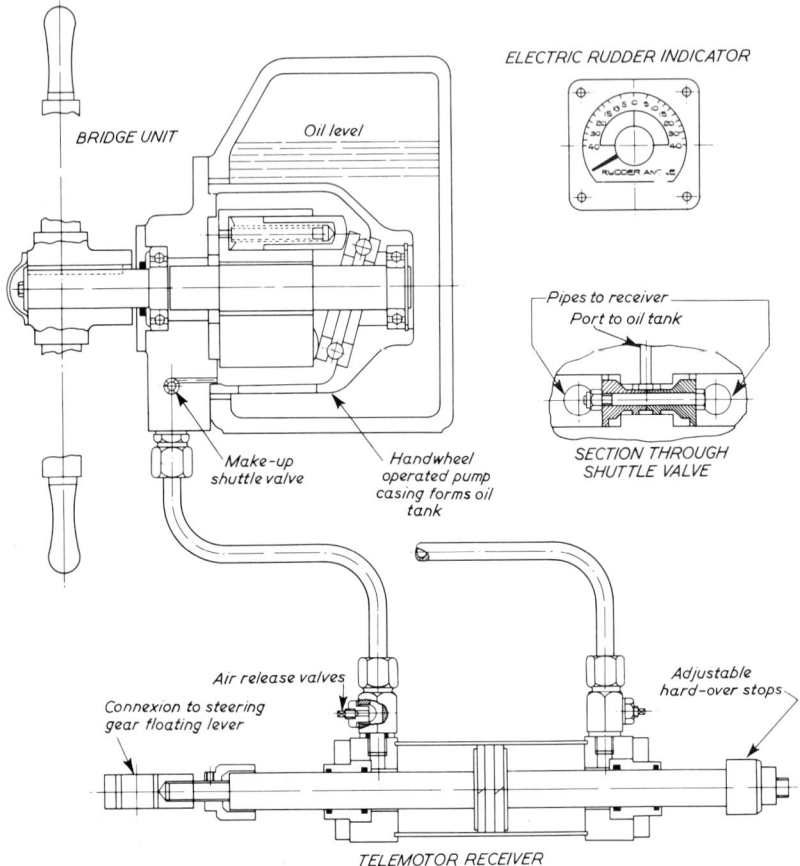

ELECTRIC RUDDER INDICATOR

BRIDGE UNIT   Oil level

Pipes to receiver
Port to oil tank

Make-up   Handwheel
shuttle valve   operated pump
                   casing forms oil
                   tank

SECTION THROUGH
SHUTTLE VALVE

Air release valves   Adjustable
                                        hard-over stops
Connexion to steering
gear floating lever

TELEMOTOR RECEIVER

FIG. 7.—*Donkin pump type telemotor and bridge unit for hand and power hydraulic steering gear.*

Because the bridge unit does not have a midship bypass, the receiver does not have midship return springs, and hence with this system of control, the steering wheel does not tend to spring back when moved from the midships position.

2.4.2. Charging

The pump type telemotor must be charged with oil and when used in conjunction with a hand and power steering gear the same oil is used throughout, because when hand steering the bridge unit transfers oil direct into and out of the main cylinders. A mineral oil with viscosity between 100 and 250 sec No. 1 Redwood at 21°C (70°F) and pour point $-29°C$ ($-20°F$) or lower is suitable.

Procedure
1) Blow through pipes with compressed air.
2) Disconnect receiver by transferring pin to Local Control.
3) Fill make up tank on top of Bridge Unit with oil.
4) Turn handwheel, opening air cock on receiver cylinder into which oil is being pumped.
5) Continue to pump until oil free of air discharges from air cock.
6) Close air cock.
7) Repeat on other side.
8) Blow air off at receiver cylinders from time to time.
9) Keep make-up tank charged with oil.

2.4.3. Checks
1) Receiver should move with two spokes turn of a large handwheel or a quarter turn of a small wheel.
2) Take wheel hardover; wheel should only move very slowly when pulled hard with receiver against stops.
3) Check for leaks at joints and glands.
4) Reconnect receiver to control and check that rudder moves in right direction under bridge control.
5) Check that rudder indicator is correctly synchronized with rudder.
6) Check that hardover stops are adjusted to operate before stops on steering gear.

2.5. ELECTRIC STEERING GEAR CONTROLS
The control methods described previously can all be applied to any type of steering gear. Basically, they are devices which convert the rotary movement of a bridge handwheel to a linear movement at the remote point where the steering gear is situated. This can then be coupled to a steam valve, hydraulic control valve, hydraulic pump stroke mechanism or electric switch. Thus, these different methods of control can be discussed in isolation from the steering gears on which they are going to be used. In the case of all electric steering gears, however, the control systems are usually part of the steering gears and are only suitable for use with the particular type of steering gear to which they are applied. Descriptions of these controls will therefore be given later with the steering gears.

2.6. NON-FOLLOW UP STEERING (OR TIME DEPENDENT STEERING)
The control systems described up to this point are all associated with "Follow up" or "Hunting Gear" systems wherein the amount of rudder angle depends upon the amount of handwheel movement. In "Non-follow up" systems, Fig. 2(e) and Fig. 8, the steering gear will move as long as the control is held in an actuating position, and will only stop when it is moved back to an "Off" position or until the steering gear has reached the hardover position. Thus, the amount of rudder movement depends upon how long

TABLE II—FAULTS, CAUSES AND REMEDIES IN PUMP TYPE TELEMOTOR OR HAND AND TOWER BRIDGE UNITS*

Fault	Cause	Remedy
1. Make up tank requires too frequent topping up.	a) External leaks in telemotor. b) External leaks in hand and power unit.	Examine pump, gyro change over valve, pipe joints and receiver glands for oil leaks. **Repair.** Examine whole steering gear for external leaks because make up tank is supply tank for whole system.
2. Wheel has too much movement before receiver responds.	a) Air in system. b) Excess clearance of shuttle valve. c) No clearance of shuttle valve.	Check that oil level has been maintained in make-up tank. Blow off air at receiver cylinders. Should be 0.8 mm ($\frac{1}{32}$ in), e.g. Fig. 6. Adjust. Prevents oil make-up and escape of air. Adjust.
3. Wheel turns too freely when pulled against handover stops.	a) External leaks. b) Internal leaks.	See 1a) and 1b). Shuttle valve not sealing properly. Examine for damage to valve and seats or foreign matter. Inspect receiver for leaking leathers or scored and worn cylinder. Examine pump for leaking valve plate or pistons.

* There are many different designs of pump type telemotor. This table is only a guide.

the control is held over and this system is therefore sometimes called "time dependent steering".

Figure 2(e) and Fig. 8 illustrate such a system. The control on the bridge is by means of a lever which is spring loaded to a central "off" position and when held to one side will give rudder movement towards port and to the other side towards starboard. The lever operates a switch which energizes one of two solenoids, depending upon the direction of movement required. These solenoids operate a pilot valve which causes the main control valve to move so as to divert oil pressure from a continuously running fixed delivery pump to the steering gear in order to give the desired direction of rudder movement. When the switch is released and springs to the central position, the control valve moves to a position where it bypasses the pump delivery, and the steering gear stops. At the same time, the control valve seals off the pipes to the main cylinders so as to hold the rudder.

Since the rudder moves as long as the control lever is held over by the helmsman, and stops moving as soon as the lever is released to spring to the "Off" position, the helmsman acts as the hunting gear, stopping rudder movement as soon as it has reached the desired angle as signalled by the rudder indicator.

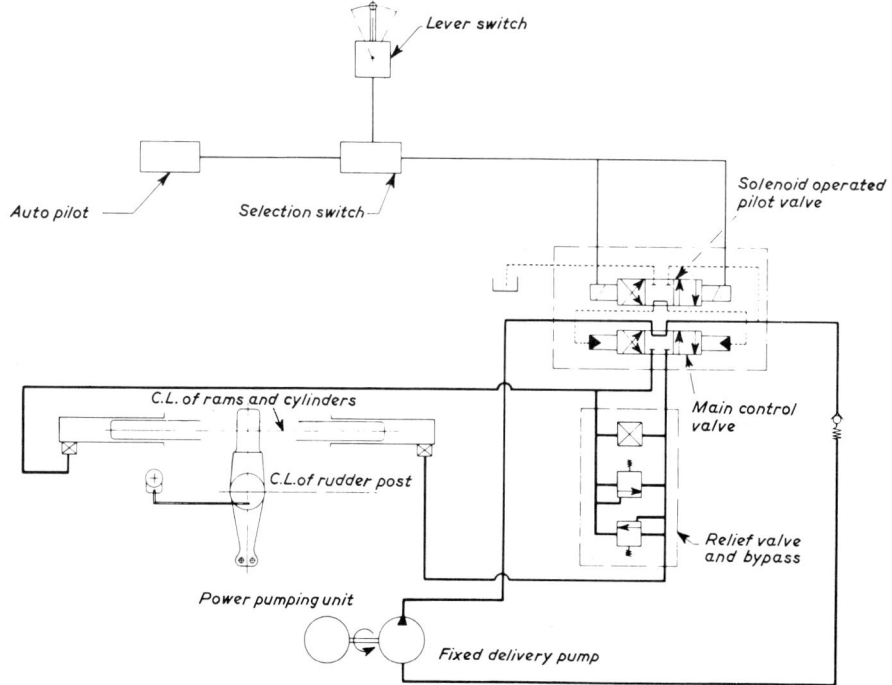

FIG. 8.—Non-follow up control diagram.

Therefore, the rudder indicator becomes an essential link in the steering gear system, and together with the helmsman completes the control loop in Fig. 2(e).

Figure 9 illustrates a special control valve assembly which provides time dependent control and is arranged to prevent uncontrolled movement of the rudder.

The valve is shown in the "cut-off" position, the passages (A) and (C) to the rudder actuator being sealed by two-part valves (E). The delivery of the power driven screw pump (S) is bypassed through passages (1) and (5) by lifting piston valve (H) against a light spring. Pilot valve (Q) is in its middle

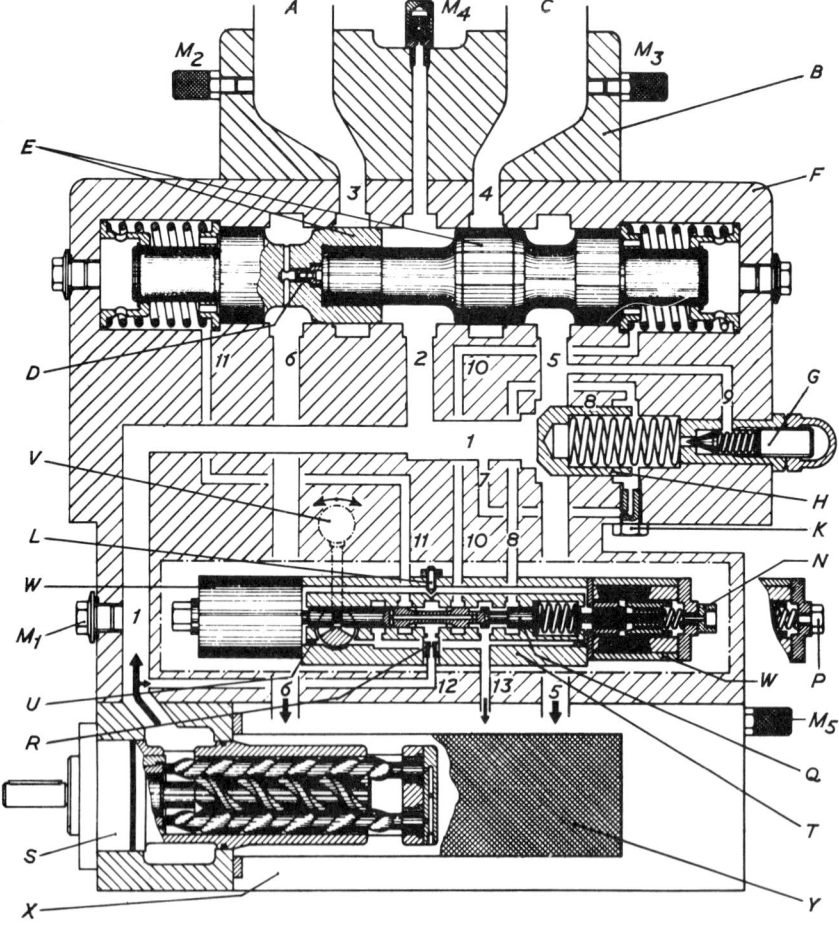

FIG. 9.—*Porsgrund control valve giving time dependent steering.*

position and can be moved by hand lever (V) or solenoids (W), so as to bring about movement of the steering gear.

When (Q) is moved to the left, port (8) is blocked and oil pressure builds up in port (7), nozzle (K), and hence behind piston valve (H) which closes. Pressure builds up through passages (12) and (11) into the left hand side of two-part control slide (E). Since there is a similar pressure in (2) both halves of (E) are forced to the right.

Because of the different areas of the valves exposed to oil pressure and larger cross section of passage (2) compared with passage (11), the right hand half of (E) moves faster than the left side. At the same time oil flow from the right hand chamber of (E) via passage (10) is throttled by pilot control slide (Q).

In this way the connexion between passages (2) and (4) are opened more quickly than those between (3) and (6). This means that the rudder cannot be moved until the oil pressure has built up close to the working pressure, preventing uncontrolled rudder movement.

As soon as the solenoid is de-energized, springs return (Q) to the middle position which opens passage (8) to tank, relieves pressure behind (H) and bypasses pump (S) at low pressure, which allows the springs to move slide valves (E) to the "cut off" position.

Relief valve (G) limits the maximum discharge pressure from the screw pump, but when the rudder is stationary slide valve (E) isolates the valve from the steering gear actuators. In these conditions it cannot therefore serve the purpose of providing relief against shock loadings on the gear brought about by the action of heavy seas on the rudder.

When an automatic helmsman is fitted, full follow up manual steering can be provided by the automatic helmsman unit, the feed back feature of the automatic helmsman functioning as hunting gear, see Section 3.3.

3. AUTOMATIC HELMSMAN

It is not intended to deal with the process by which the bridge unit of the automatic helmsman receives its instructions to change course (Figs. 2(c), (e) and (f), but only to show how the unit links into the steering gear control.

At first the automatic helmsman was placed alongside the steering wheel column and could be clutched in to operate it instead of the human helmsman. This method is still used to steer ships with hand-only steering.

It has been the practice for many years for the automatic helmsman to have its own power unit. This is located at the steering engine control, to which signals from the bridge unit are transmitted.

3.1. ELECTRO–MECHANICAL POWER UNIT

Figure 10 represents the type of electro-mechanical power unit used in conjunction with the earlier forms of automatic helmsman in which the control unit was housed in a column separate from the hydraulic telemotor. The bridge unit is provided with a control lever with three positions, "Off", "Hand" and "Gyro". In the "Off" position, the automatic helmsman is out of action; in the "Hand" position the pilot wheel can be used for manual control of the steering gear; and in the "Gyro" position, automatic steering is engaged. When the control lever is in the "Hand" or "Gyro" positions, a bypass valve on the hydraulic telemotor transmitter must be opened so that the telemotor receiver can move freely. The power unit is linked to the steering gear control and comprises a drive motor, rack, magnetic clutch, limit switches, the synchro transmitter and gear trains. The motor is a reversible machine fed direct from the ship's mains and, to ensure that it stops quickly when a signal is cancelled, dynamic braking is utilized. The motor drives the rack through gearing and an electro-magnetic clutch, the rack being coupled to the steering gear control. The clutch is necessary in the power unit so that the motor and rack will be disconnected when the gyro pilot is not in use. The rack will then move freely when the hydraulic telemotor is being employed.

The coil of the electro-magnetic clutch is connected through a control switch, operated by the control lever, the circuit being completed only when the control lever is in the "Hand" or "Gyro" position. In this case, "Hand" refers to the handwheel on the automatic helmsman and not hand operation

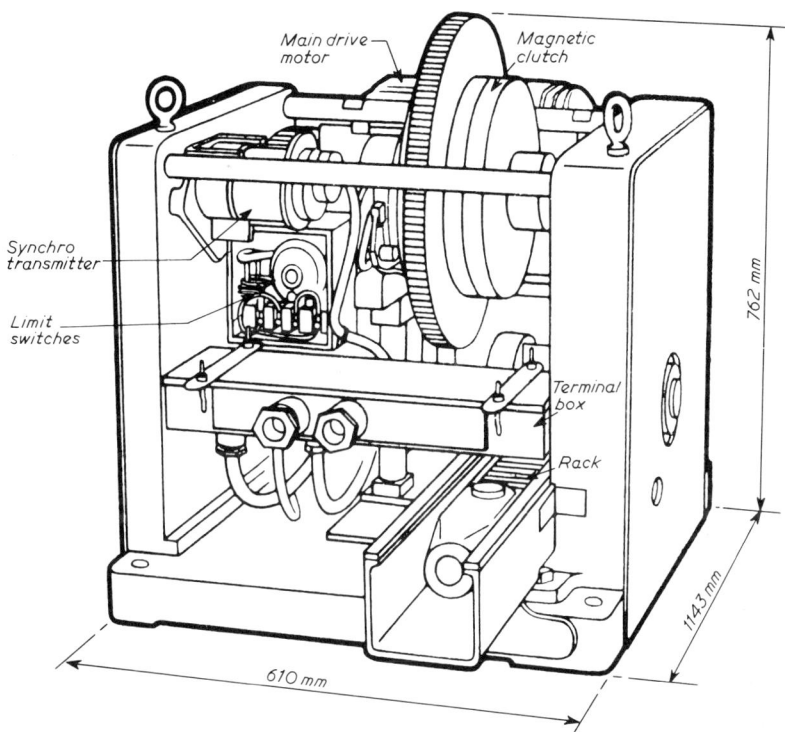

FIG. 10.—*Electro–mechanical auto pilot power unit.*

by means of the hydraulic telemotor. The clutch also acts as a safety device, being designed to slip under excessive torque load.

The limit switches in the power unit are operated by cams turned through gearing by the movement of the rack. These switches are set to trip in the hardover positions inside the stops on the telemotor receiver and are so arranged that when a limit switch has been tripped in one direction, no further movement can be made in that direction. However, the unit will respond to a reverse signal.

In many of these early installations there was no safety switch coupled to the lever operating the bypass on the telemotor. Thus, in such installations it is most important to see that this lever is placed in the "Gyro" position before switching on the gyro unit. The reason for this is that if the steering control was operated by the gyro unit, the handwheel on the telemotor could be caused to rotate by drive-back from the telemotor receiver which could cause injury to personnel and excessive hydraulic pressures in the system. Equally, if the hydraulic telemotor were operated with the gyro unit switched on, although there is a slipping clutch in the gyro power unit (which is designed to slip under excessive load), excessive pressures could be built up in the hydraulic system before the clutch would slip.

3.2. Electro–Hydraulic Power Unit

It is current practice to use an electro–hydraulic method for driving the steering gear control instead of the electro-mechanical method just described.

This is illustrated by the schematic diagram in Fig. 11 from which it is seen that control impulses from the automatic helmsman are directed, via the control and power amplifiers, to operate solenoids coupled to a hydraulic directional control valve. This valve, working in conjunction with a separate hydraulic power unit, directs hydraulic fluid to one side or other of the piston in a receiver assembly, which is similar in principle to those already described

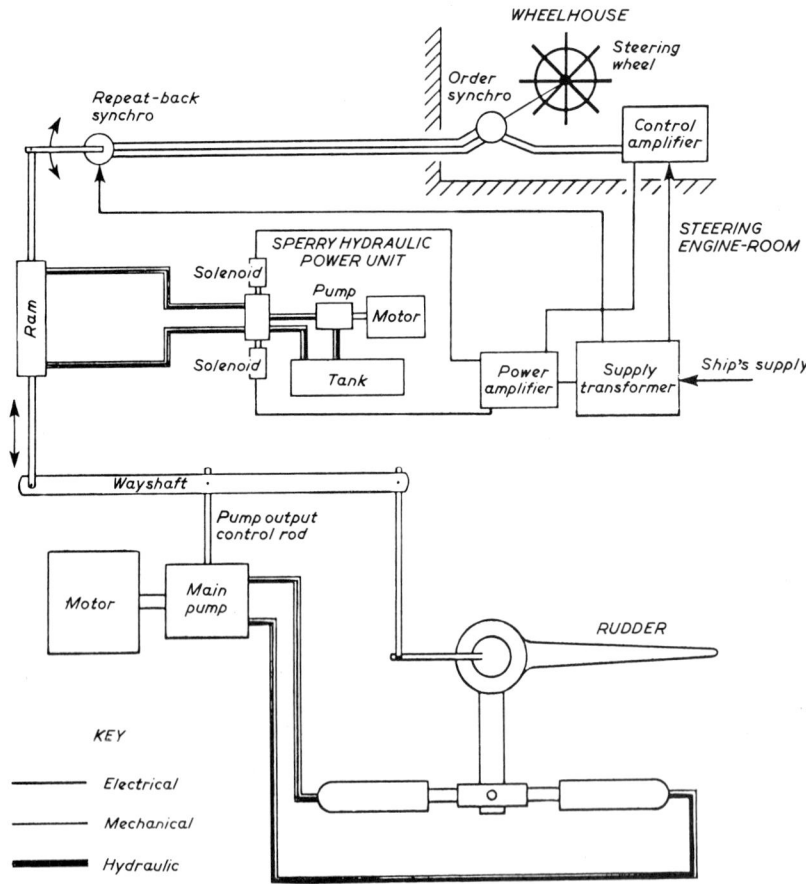

Fig. 11.—*Electro–hydraulic auto pilot power unit.*

in the hydraulic telemotor control systems. This assembly then acts through a hunting control gear in the same manner as a telemotor receiver, thereby causing the main steering gear rams and the rudder to move to the new position dictated by the automatic helmsman. It is also coupled to a repeat back synchro unit which is designed to cancel the original control signal from the automatic helmsman as soon as the required helm angle has been applied.

Modern practice is to combine the telemotor and automatic helmsman bridge unit in one column Fig. 6.

3.3. DUPLEX AUTOMATIC HELMSMAN

Alternatively, the automatic helmsman can be used alone without a hydraulic telemotor. In addition to automatic control of steering, the unit is provided with a handwheel for manual control with full follow up characteristics using the feed back of the automatic helmsman as hunting gear.

The same hand wheel can be used as a right- and left-hand switch operating the auxiliary controller shown in Fig. 12 to give non-follow-up steering in the event of any failure in the servo controlled loop. This control is also used to provide the completely independent control from the bridge required by the Rules (Section 1.1.1.). As will be seen from Fig. 12, the hydraulic control rams, solenoid operated power units and electricity supply circuits are duplicated in order to meet this requirement. The rudder indicator informs the helmsman when he has moved the rudder to the desired angle, when he releases the handwheel which is sprung to the "Off" position. Figure 2(e) illustrates the emergency control, while 2(f) illustrates how the feed back of the automatic helmsman can give hunting gear characteristics to a non-follow up type steering gear.

3.4. DUPLICATE ELECTRICAL CONTROL

A more recent development in steering gear control is shown at Fig. 13. As with the duplex system, a hydraulic telemotor is dispensed with but, in addition, the need for the solenoid controlled pumps—with their hydraulic receivers and mechanical linkage and hunting gear on the steering gear—is eliminated. This simplification is obtained by means of an electrical torque motor which is directly coupled to the control slide valve of the hydraulic steering gear pump. Electrical control signals from the bridge are directed to the torque motor, which actuates the slide valve and this, in turn, controls the output of the pump so as to move the rudder. When the steering gear has attained the required rudder angle, the electric feedback unit connected direct to the rudder stock cancels the input signal to the control amplifier and the steering gear is held at that angle until another rudder movement is required.

With this system, the response time from helm demand to movement of the steering gear is greatly decreased and the accuracy of the rudder position improved. Duplication of the electrical controls as required by the Rules is

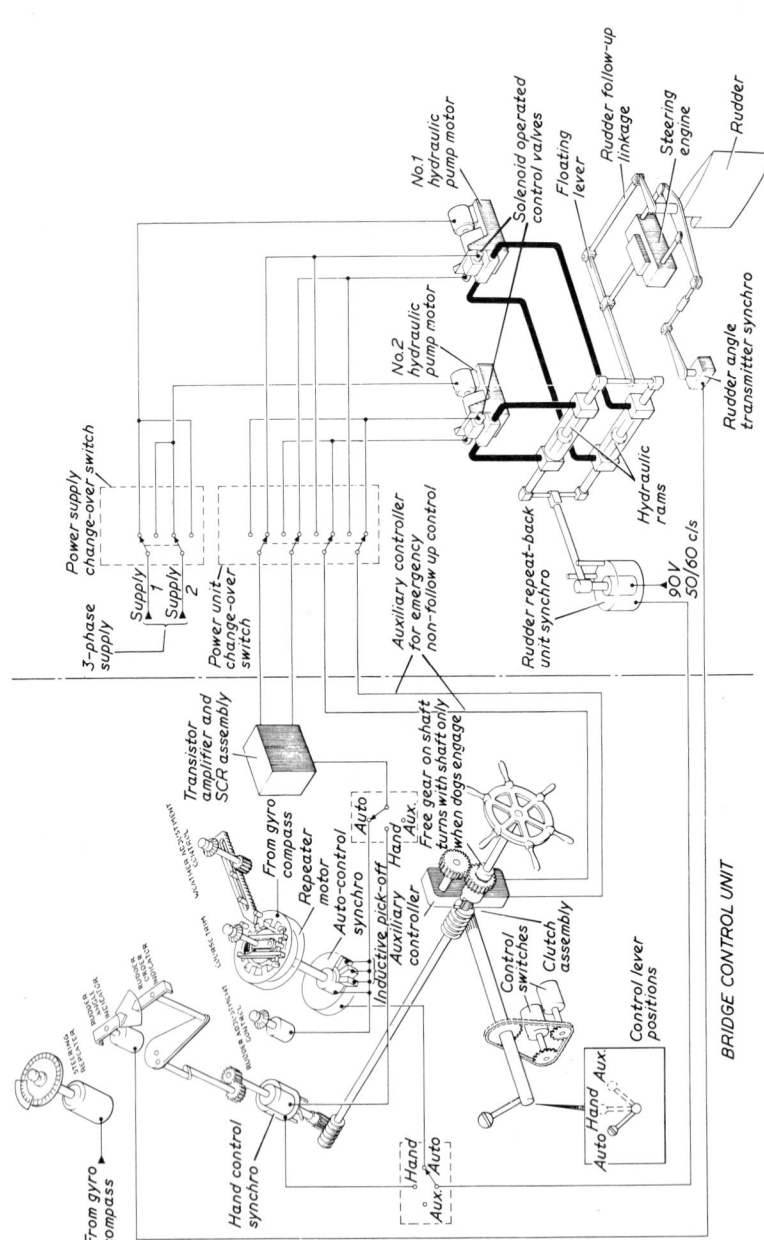

FIG. 12.—Duplex control automatic helmsman.

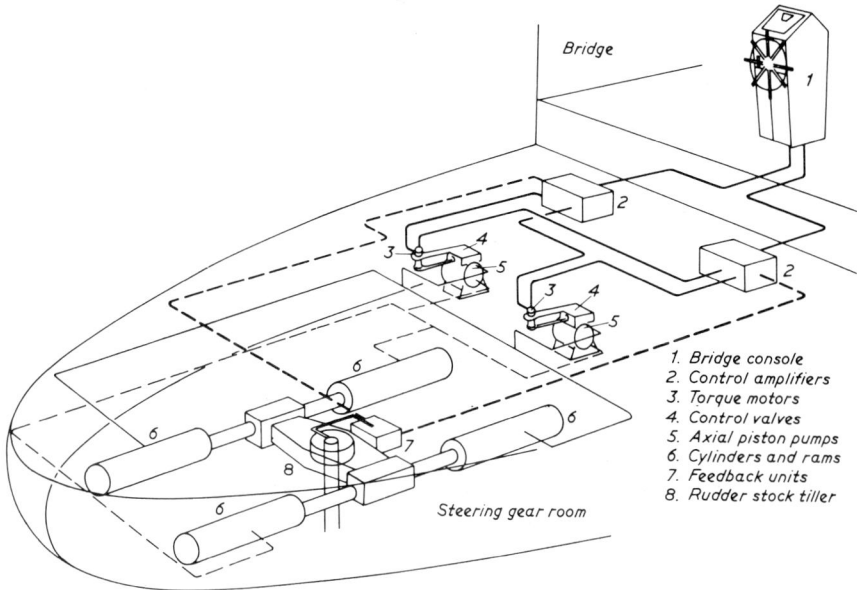

1. Bridge console
2. Control amplifiers
3. Torque motors
4. Control valves
5. Axial piston pumps
6. Cylinders and rams
7. Feedback units
8. Rudder stock tiller

FIG. 13.—*Hastie single loop control system.*

provided and it is also possible in an emergency for non follow up control to be effected. Figures 2(e) and 2(f) apply also to this steering gear control system, (Figure 24 shows the external control arrangements on the high pressure servo controlled axial piston pump for which this control system is designed.)

4. STEAM STEERING GEAR

While steam steering gears operate in many ships still in service it is some years since any have been supplied for new tonnage. For this reason, only a very brief description will be given with notes on some of the points to watch on machines which have been subject to considerable wear.

4.1. CHAIN GEARS

For many years it was common practice to place the steering engine on the bridge or upper part of the engine room and couple it to the rudder stock with rods and chains, bends being negotiated by passing the chains round sheaves. Buffer springs in the chain lead cushioned shocks. Because of the proximity of the engine to the bridge, helm orders were transmitted to the engine by shafting and bevel wheels.

This provided a very inexpensive installation, but persistent failures due to damage to the chain leads led to this combination giving way to designs where the engine was directly coupled to the rudder stock. The proved reliability of the hydraulic telemotor for the more remote control involved facilitating this change.

4.2. WILSON–PIRRIE GEAR

The Wilson–Pirrie drive shown in Fig. 14 was the method most commonly adopted for steam engines. The engine drives a pinion (5) through a worm (L) and wheel (6). The pinion gears into quadrant (2) which is connected to the tiller (1) by buffer springs (3), the tiller being keyed to the rudder stock and the quadrant free on the stock, but keywayed for emergency purposes.

The engine has two double-acting cylinders with cranks at right angles and distributing valves without Lap or Lead. This enables the engine to start up in any position and in either direction depending on which sides are connected to the steam and exhaust by the control valve, respectively. With the pistons (A) and (B) in the positions shown, it will be appreciated that piston (B) alone can exert any useful torque. In addition, since steam is admitted for the full piston stroke and the same amount of steam is used for a given angular rudder movement whether maximum or even negative torque is being overcome, this is a very uneconomical engine.

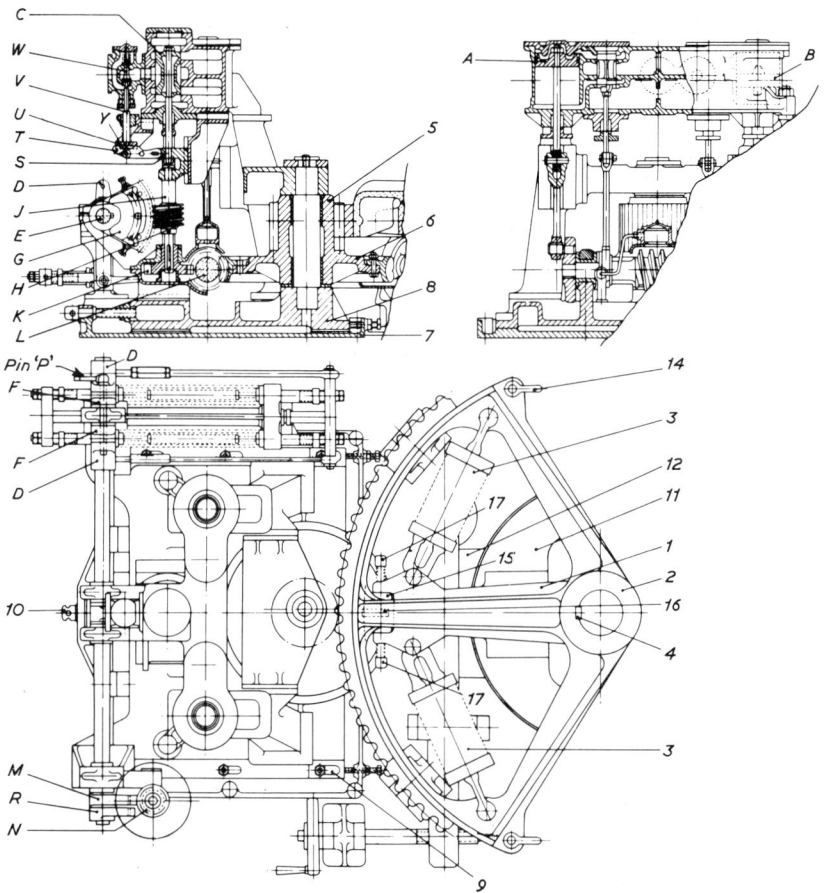

FIG. 14.—*Wilson–Pirrie steam gear.*

4.2.1. Hunting Gear

The control valve (*C*) is operated by the helm and hunting gear. When at rest, the control valve bars seal the steam and exhaust lines from the engine. Helm movement pivots weighbar shaft (*E*), which through toothed quadrant (*G*) and worm (*H*) raises or lowers valve (*C*) admitting steam to the engine to give port or starboard rudder movement as ordered.

As the engine runs it returns the control valve to the cut off position through the hunting gear mechanism. This consists of cut off wheel (*K*) which is rotated by the main worm (*L*). (*K*) rotates worm shaft (*J*) through sliding keys. Worm (*H*) screws itself up or down on the teeth of quadrant (*G*) so as to move control valve (*C*) back to "Cut Off".

4.3. Steam Hydraulic Steering Gear

A number of these gears were fitted during the 1950's to tankers having the necessary auxiliary steam supply and Fig. 15 illustrates one such design. A reversible steam engine drives a variable stroke hydraulic pump to supply pressure oil to the rudder actuating cylinders.

The pump is of the Hele–Shaw type similar to that described later in Section 6.3. The stroke however is controlled by a spring which normally holds full stroke on the pump. Opposing this spring are rams in two small cylinders A and B shown in the section at XX Fig. 15, each of which is connected to one of the main cylinders. At the low pressures prevalent when the rudder is near midships, full stroke is maintained. As the pressure rises in either main cylinder to about half the maximum pressure, the appropriate ram begins to compress the spring, so reducing the pump stroke progressively until, at maximum pressure, a stop is reached set at $\frac{1}{4}$ of full stroke.

Reversal of pumping results when the engine reverses, and the engine and pump only run when it is desired to move the rudder. Thus, in effect, the engine is coupled to the rudder through a gear ratio which automatically

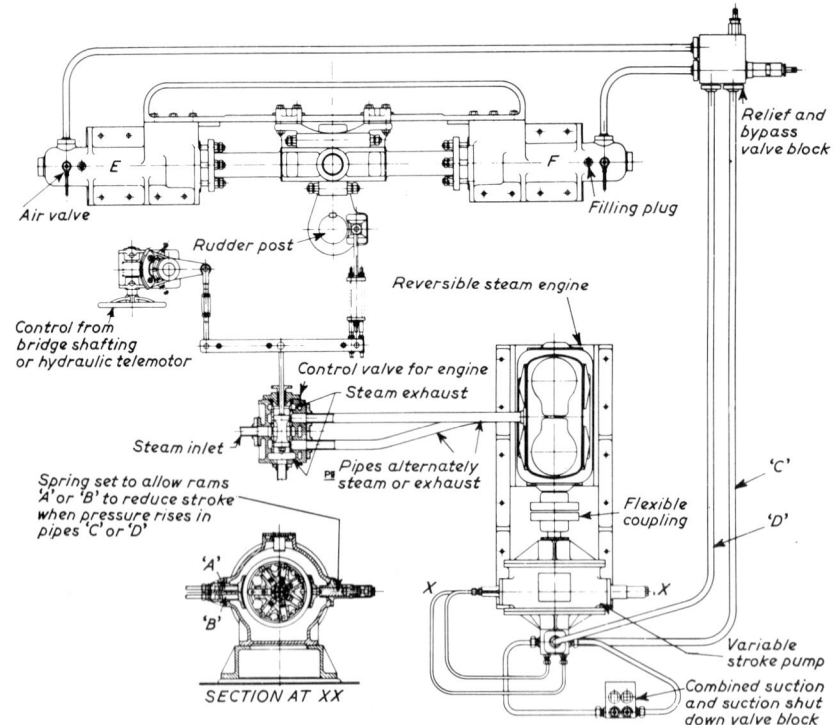

Fig. 15.—*Donkin steam hydraulic steering gear.*

TABLE III—FAULTS, CAUSES AND REMEDIES IN STEAM STEERING GEAR

Fault	Cause	Remedy
1. Too much steering wheel movement required before engine moves.	a) Fault in control system.	Check that no undue lost motion in control (see Table 1, 3 and 4).
	b) Economic valve.	Wear of operating cams would cause delay in admission of steam. Adjust clearance.
	c) Accumulation of water in steam line.	Drains should be kept cracked so that water drains off as it forms. If steam trap fitted check adjustment.
	d) Excessive lap on control valve.	Correct.
2. Engine running too slowly.	a) Steam supply inadequate.	Check reducing valve. Supply to engine should be 7 bar (100 lb/in²) should not drop below 5 bar (70 lb/in²) with engine running.
	b) Back pressure in exhaust line.	Can be caused by other auxiliaries exhausting into steering gear pipe line. Steering gear should have exclusive pipe lines.
	c) Mechanical overload in engine.	This could be due to friction. e.g. from seizing rudder stock bearing, engine worm shaft or quarter block in case of chain gear.
	d) The engine may be worn.	Renew piston rings if gaps 1·5 mm (0·60 in—initially 0·025 in). rebore cylinders and fit new pistons if 0·38 mm–0·51 mm (0·015–0·020 in) wear. Renew control valve if 0·15 mm (0·006 in) clearance. Distributing valves if 0·20 mm (0·008 in) clearance. Rebore valve chests if oval. When adjusting eccentric bearings readjust height of distributing valves. With piston at dead centre valve should just cover ports.
3. Vibrations at midships.	Some rudders vibrate badly at midships and cause vibrations and slamming at the steering gear.	Pinions and quadrant teeth on Wilson–Pirrie gears can usually be engaged firmly at midships if they have knuckle teeth and the makers have kept centre segment tooth proud of other teeth. Worm shaft thrust clearance should not be allowed to become excessive. Chains should be kept adjusted so that no undue slack.
4. Buffer springs between quadrant and tiller Wilson–Pirrie gear not working in service.	Quadrant boss seized on rudder post.	Must be kept lubricated.

adjusts itself to the required torque. This enables rudder movements for small rudder angles to be made rapidly and with relatively few engine revolutions, while the engine speeds up to produce greater horsepower under high torque conditions. With this arrangement, a steering engine can be used of capacity only one quarter of that required when directly coupled, resulting in substantial savings in cost and steam consumption.

In alternative designs of steam hydraulic steering gear, the engine and pump run continuously in one direction, the pump being stroked in opposite directions to cause reverse rudder movement in the same manner as electric motor drive.

In one design, the engine speed is controlled by a governor, and in another a throttling valve is actuated together with the pump stroke so that full steam is admitted for more major rudder movements; but when no stroke is on the pump, and the rudder is not moving, then only sufficient steam passes to keep the engine ticking over.

5. DIRECT ELECTRIC STEERING GEAR

Only electrical power units are used with these systems. These gears, which operate from d.c. supply, generally fall into two groups, namely the Ward–Leonard Systems and the Contactor Operated Single Motor Systems. Both groups use the Wilson–Pirrie principle for the drive, a toothed quadrant on the rudder stock being driven by a rudder motor to which it is geared through worm gearing and a pinion.

5.1. WARD–LEONARD SYSTEM

Figure 16 shows a diagram of a Ward–Leonard steering gear. In this example, a Wheatstone Bridge method of control is used.

A motor generator set which runs continuously at sea has a direct coupled exciter which provides the field current of the generator. Control is carried out on the field of the exciter, and thus comparatively small currents have to be handled for control purposes. Some manufacturers, however, omit the exciter and exercise control on the field winding of the generator. The use of an exciter is largely determined by the magnitude of the field current of the generator and whether or not high torques are required.

When the control system is at rest, there is no voltage across the exciter shunt field, no output from the exciter and no current in the shunt field of the generator. Thus, there is no output from the generator, although it is continuously running, and the main rudder motor, connected to the rudder head, does not turn.

When the controller is offset a voltage is impressed across the exciter field, the exciter generates a voltage which causes current to flow in the field coils of the generator, and the generator then supplies a voltage to the main rudder motor which rotates. The speed of the main rudder motor varies with the voltage supplied to it by the generator and the generator voltage will vary according to the potential difference across the exciter shunt field.

As the steering wheel is moved, the contact on the wheelhouse rheostat is offset and a difference of potential exists across the exciter field, causing the main rudder to rotate. When the rudder has moved the requisite amount, the contact on the rudder rheostat will have moved to a position coincident with the wheelhouse rheostat contact, so that the exciter shunt field again has zero volts across it. Rotation of the main rudder motor ceases and the system comes to rest. The movement of the contact on the rudder rheostat

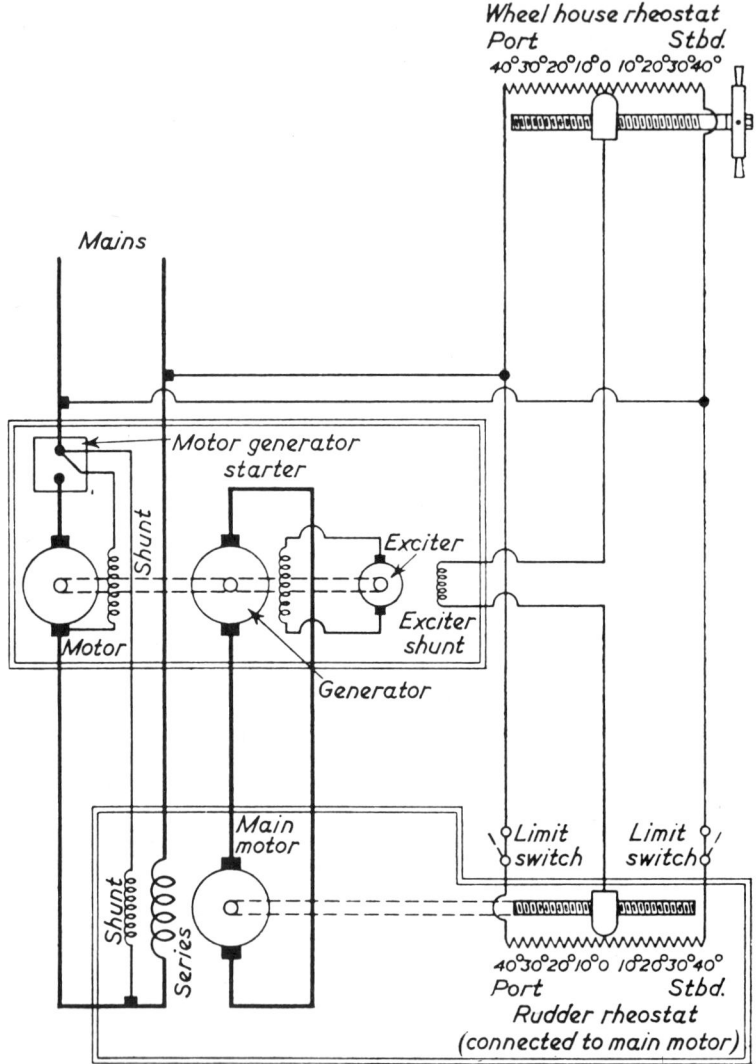

Fig. 16.—*Ward–Leonard electric steering gear.*

serves a similar purpose to the hunting gear on steam and electro hydraulic steering gears and so full "Follow Up" type control of the steering gear is provided.

Such an arrangement gives sensitive control and for large movements, high torque and faster initial movement which decreases as the two rheostats come into coincidence. Thus the motor starts smoothly, accelerates to a maximum then decelerates until it stops smoothly.

The rudder rheostat often has slightly more travel than the wheelhouse rheostat, so that when the latter is hard over, the rudder still has further to go. Limit switches are fitted to prevent over run but are connected so that when they operate the exciter field is reversed. This causes the rudder motor to reverse so bringing the rudder back from the stops.

5.2. SINGLE MOTOR SYSTEM

Figure 17 is a simplified wiring diagram for a single motor gear. As with the Ward–Leonard system, a d.c. motor is mechanically coupled through gearing to the rudder head but in this case the motor is compounded within a predominently series field power supply taken direct from the ship's main supply through a contactor type starter. The starter is fitted with reversing contacts so as to give port or starboard movements in response to movements of the helm. On large installations, series resistors are incorporated in the starting mechanism in order to limit the starting currents and these are cut out automatically and sequentially by contactors using time lag devices.

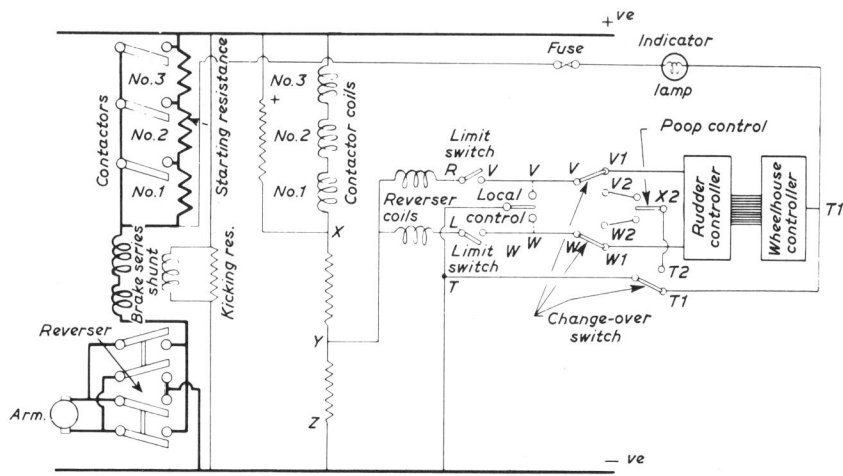

FIG. 17.—*Single motor electric steering gear.*

Because the motor runs at full speed to the point of cut off by the control, a magnetic brake is required and this ensures that when coincidence is reached between helm and rudder the rudder comes quickly to rest at the new helm angle without overrun taking place.

5.2.1. Electric Telemotor

The telemotor consists of a spiral of contacts on the bridge arranged so that each contact corresponds with a position of the handwheel. Connexions from these contacts are run by means of multi-core cable to similar contacts on a receiver unit which is connected to and rotated by the steering gear motor. As the receiver unit comes to coincidence with the telemotor on the bridge, the control circuits of the starter contactors are opened so that the rudder motor is stopped and the brake immediately applied. As in the case of the Wheatstone Bridge control this acts as a hunting gear so as to provide "Follow Up" control of the steering gear.

5.3. Maintenance

Normal electrical maintenance is required on the electrical equipment, such as attention to commutators and contactors. After many years of service, the sliding contacts of the Ward–Leonard rheostats and the contact fingers of the single motor telemotors will need renewal if wear down has lessened the spring tension which holds the contact faces together.

The worm and worm wheel drive for electrical steering gears are normally totally enclosed and provided with oil bath type lubrication so that little wear, if any, takes place in this type of drive.

All electric steering gears have shown themselves to be very reliable but their higher cost (due to the special electrical equipment they involve) as compared with the equally reliable hydraulic gear has led to their being superseded on new tonnage by electro–hydraulic steering gears. However, there are a number of ships at sea in which all electric steering gears continue to give good service.

6. HYDRAULIC STEERING GEAR

A hydraulic steering gear consists of a bridge control which applies helm, an engine control which is operated jointly by the helm and hunting gear (when fitted) and a power pump and rudder actuator which constitutes the steering engine.

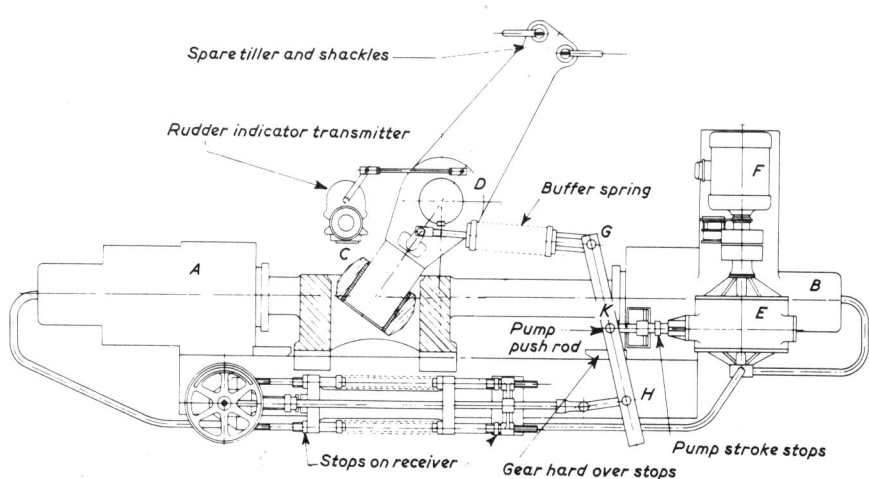

Spare tiller and shackles

Rudder indicator transmitter

Buffer spring

Pump push rod

Stops on receiver

Gear hard over stops

Pump stroke stops

FIG. 18.—*Action of hunting gear and mechanical advantage of Rapson slide.*

6.1. HUNTING GEAR

Figure 18 shows a typical arrangement. The rudder actuator consists of two cylinders (*A*) and (*B*) the rams from which engage tiller (*C*) keyed to rudder stock (*D*). A variable stroke reversible pump (*E*) is driven by electric motor (*F*). The pump stroke push rod is pinned to the central point (*K*) of the floating lever. One end (*H*) of the floating lever is connected to the telemotor receiver and moves in response to helm orders, while the other end (*G*) is linked to and moves in response to tiller movements thus forming the hunting gear.

In the position shown, if the helm is turned towards midships, the telemotor receiver will move (*H*) and hence (*K*) to the left as the floating lever pivots about (*G*). This will put stroke on the pump which will draw oil from cylinder (*B*) and pump it into cylinder (*A*) which will move the tiller towards midships and end (*G*) of the floating lever to the right until it returns the pump push rod to the no stroke position when movement will stop and the rudder angle will correspond to the helm angle. See Figs. 2(b), (c) and (d).

The buffer spring (*L*) in the hunting gear link can take up excess movement should the helmsman apply a signal which moves the floating lever beyond the maximum stroke position. The extra movement is stored by compressing the spring which resets itself as the hunting gear approaches coincidence.

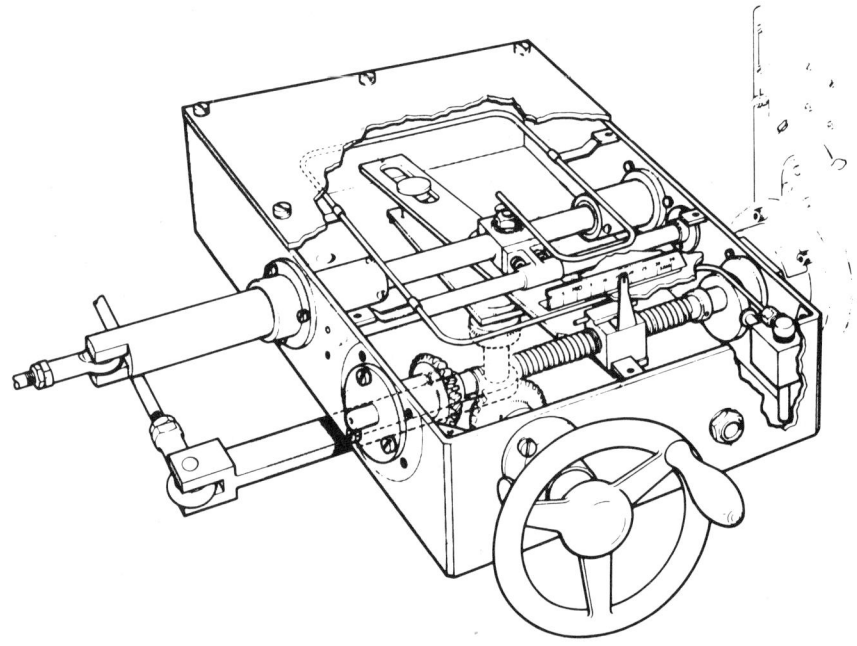

FIG. 19.—*Brown Bros. miniaturised hunting gear.*

Where servo controlled pumps are used the effort to operate the pump control mechanism is small so that the hunting control gear can be miniaturised and built into a totally enclosed "lubricated for life" box. Figure 19 shows one such unit as used by Brown Bros. on their four cylinder Rapson slide steering gear. The control unit in this case is designed to accept electrical signals only from the bridge but similar designs can be arranged to accept hydraulic signals. The external connexions to the box are (i) the rotary actuator which accepts the electrical signal from the bridge (ii) the pump stroke rods, one for each pump, (iii) the cut-off rod from the rudder and (iv) a local control handwheel.

Hydraulic power can be converted into torque at the rudder stock by a number of different actuator designs. There are also a number of different pumps and ways of diverting the output of the pumps to the actuators. Any of the pumping units can be used in conjunction with any of the actuators.

6.2. PUMPING UNITS

These can be of either the variable capacity reversible delivery type or the fixed delivery non-reversible type. For the larger outputs with high rates of change in demand the variable capacity pumps are normally fitted. These are of two types, the Hele–Shaw variable stroke pump having radial cylinders and the swashplate variable stroke pump having axial cylinders.

6.3. HELE–SHAW PUMP

Figure 20 illustrates the construction and operation of this type of pump which is normally driven by a constant speed electric motor. It consists of a case A to which are attached two covers, the shaft cover B and the pipe connexion cover C. This latter cover carries the D tube (or central valve), which has ports E and F forming the connexions between the cylinders and branches G and H. The cylinder body J is driven by shaft K, and revolves on the D tube, being supported at either end by ball bearings T. The pistons L are fitted in a row of radial cylinders and through the outer end of each piston is a gudgeon pin M, which attaches the slippers N to the piston. The slippers are free to oscillate on their gudgeon pins and fit into tracks in the circular floating ring O. This ring is free to rotate being mounted on ball

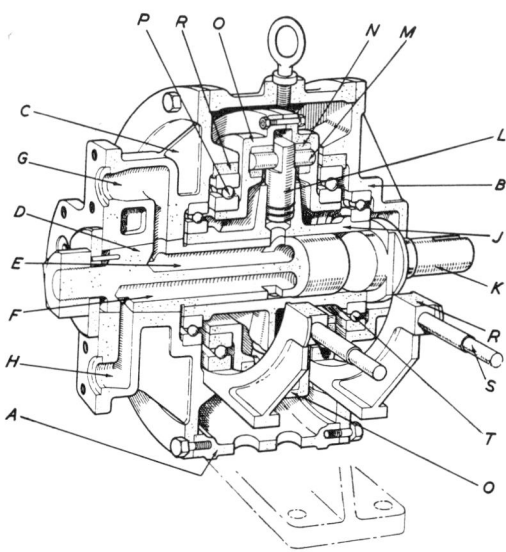

FIG. 20.—*Hele–Shaw type variable stroke pump.*

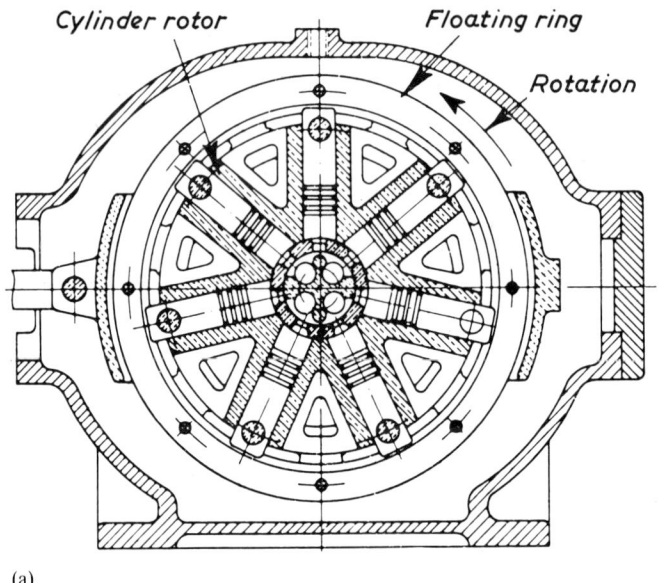

(a)

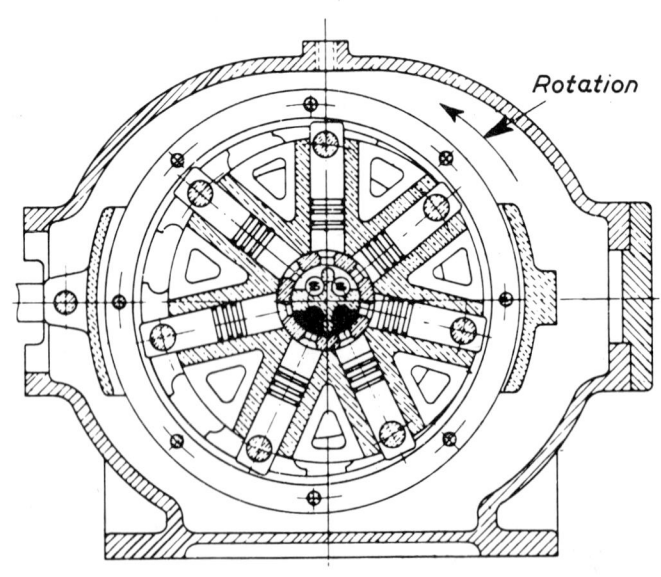

(b)

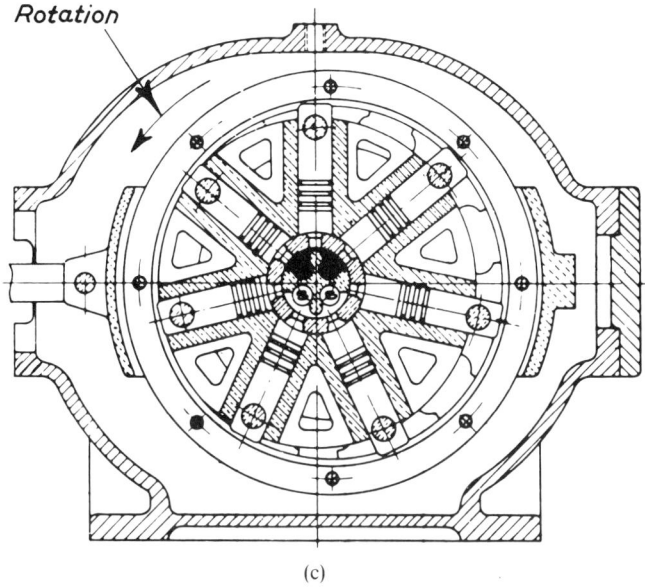

Rotation

(c)

FIG. 21.—*Variable stroke Hele–Shaw pump in three different working positions* (a) *Neutral position;* (b) *Full stroke—port delivery;* (c) *Full stroke—starboard delivery.*

bearings *P*, which are housed in guide blocks *R*. The latter bear on tracks formed on the covers *B* and *C* and are controlled in their movement by spindles *S*, which pass through the pump case *A*. The movement of the floating ring *O* by control spindles *S* from a central position causes pistons *L* to reciprocate in the radial cylinders so that a pumping action takes place. The direction of pumping depends upon whether the movement is to left or right of the central position and this is illustrated in Fig. 21.

6.4. SUCTION VALVES

Oil leaking past the centre valve and plungers drains through the casing into a tank below the pumps. Replenishment oil can be sucked from this tank through pipes which connect it to the main system, past non-return suction valves.

6.5. AUXILIARY PUMP

Some manufacturers supply an auxiliary pump driven from the main pump shaft, which draws oil from the replenishment tank, delivering through non-return valves to each side of the main hydraulic system. A low pressure relief valve opens to return the auxiliary pump delivery back to the replenishment tank if the main system is full, at the same time keeping equivalent initial pressure on the whole system. This ensures the lubrication of the main pumps when at no stroke and resists the ingress of air into the system.

Pressure from this pump can also be used to power the automatic helmsman control, to operate change over valves (see Section 6.9), or to power servo control units which in large installations may be used to operate pump stroke mechanisms and so reduce the force required from the telemotor.

6.6. VARIABLE STROKE REVERSIBLE SWASHPLATE PUMP

This pump runs in the flooded condition, the make-up tank being above the level of the pump so that all the working parts are immersed in oil. It is driven by a constant speed electric motor, the volume and direction of the oil flow being controlled by means of a stroke control lever.

One such pump in common use is that shown in Fig. 22. The cylinders are formed in the cylinder barrel (4) which is held in contact with the film face on the valve plate (5) by hydraulic pressure, initial contact being maintained by a spring (14). Each piston (11) is formed with a ball end fitted into a socket (21) the bearing face of these sockets and the film faces being a lapped finish and of a special design to reduce the hydraulic loading on the mating surfaces. These mating faces and also the valve plate and swashplate (3) take the axial loading of the pump.

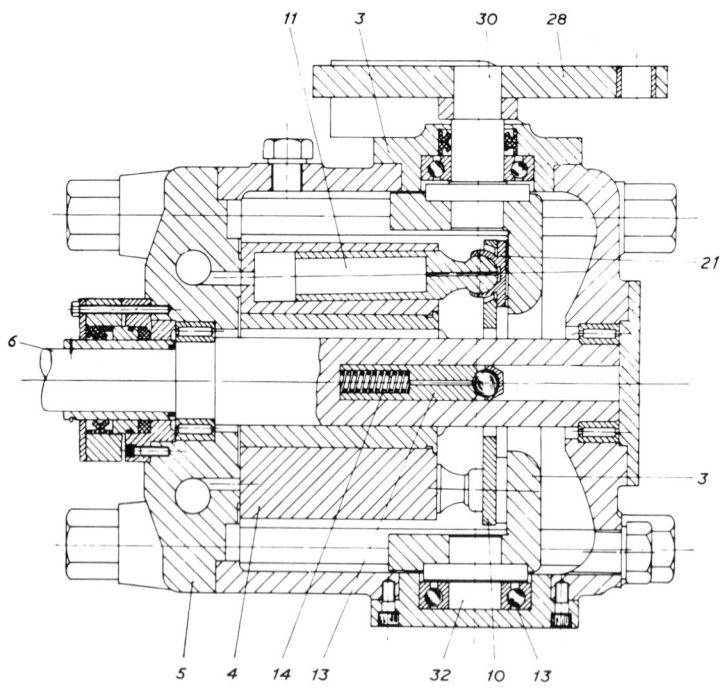

FIG. 22.—*Donkin variable stroke swashplate pump.*

The cylinder block (4), spring (14), mandrel (13) and the retracting plate (10) rotate in unison with the driving shaft (6). Bolted to the swashplate (3) are the swashplate trunnions (30) and (32) which in turn are mounted in ball bearings housed in the casing. The top trunnion is extended through the top of the casing. An oil seal above the bearing keeps it oiltight. On the extended end of the trunnion is keyed the control lever (28), which is operated by the steering gear control mechanism.

When the lever is in neutral position the face of the swashplate is at 90° to the driving shaft and consequently the piston shoes revolving with the pistons and the cylinder block and bearing against the face of the swashplate have no lateral movement and no oil is being pumped. When the control lever is moved, the angle of the swashplate is altered and the pistons and shoes begin reciprocating through the attached shoes sliding up or down the inclined planes formed by the altered angle of the swashplate. According to the way and to what angle the swashplate is tilted, so is the amount and direction of oil pumped controlled.

Ports in the cylinders communicate alternately with two semi-circular ports in the valve plate (5) so that oil can be drawn in and discharged from the pump through pipes connected to the valve plate and cover, the direction of flow depending on the slope of the swashplate in the manner described.

The V.S.G. type pump shown in Fig. 23 has been in common use for many years. The main difference between this pump and the "slipper pad" pump already described is in the method of driving the pistons. The pistons (E) are hollow so as to accommodate a spherical seat into which the ball end of connecting rod (D) engages. The other end of the rod is held in one of a ring of sockets (N) which is driven round with cylinder barrel (F) by driving shaft (A) through a universal joint (M). The socket ring is pressed back against the tilt box (B) by spring and hydraulic pressure, roller bearings (C) transmitting the thrust load.

The pumps so far described operate with maximum pressures in the range 96–138 bar (1400–2000 lb/in²), but in recent years new designs of the axial piston type have been developed which operate at higher speeds and with maximum pressures in the range 207–276 bar (3000–4000 lb/in²). Two such pumps coming into general use with different manufacturers are the Vickers Sunstrand pump and a Hastie pump recently developed in conjunction with the National Engineering Laboratory. Each of these pumps uses a servo system for the operation of the swashplate so that the steering control effort is very much reduced. Figure 24 shows the Hastie high pressure pump and the control arrangement to which reference is made in Section 3.4.

6.7. FIXED DELIVERY PUMPS

While variable stroke pumps are usually specially made for steering gear duty, fixed delivery pumps can be production line proprietary models, and gear pumps, vane pumps, screw pumps or ram pumps of standard form

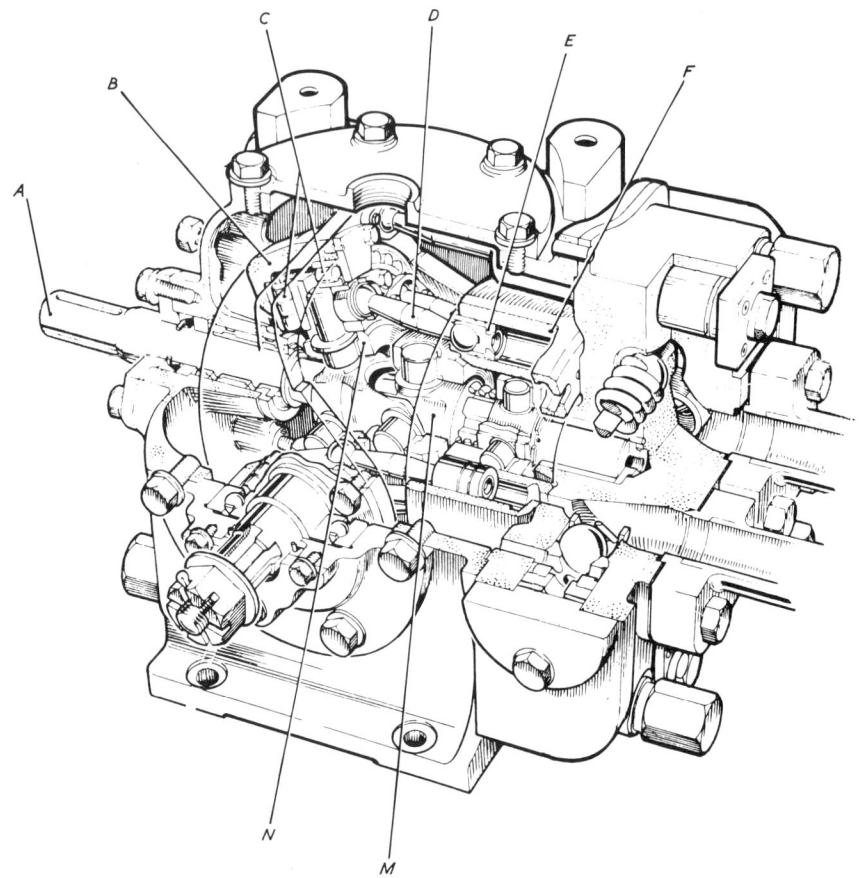

FIG. 23.—*V.S.G. swashplate pump.*

are used. As the operation of such pumps is a matter of general engineering knowledge no detailed descriptions are given here.

6.7.1. Control Valve and Hunting Gear—(Fig. 2(d))

Since the pump delivers a uniform volume of oil continuously in one direction, control is achieved by using an open centred four-way control valve, as shown diagrammatically in Fig. 25. The valve spindle is connected to the central point of the floating lever, one end of which is connected to telemotor receiver and the other end to a link incorporating a buffer spring attached to the tiller.

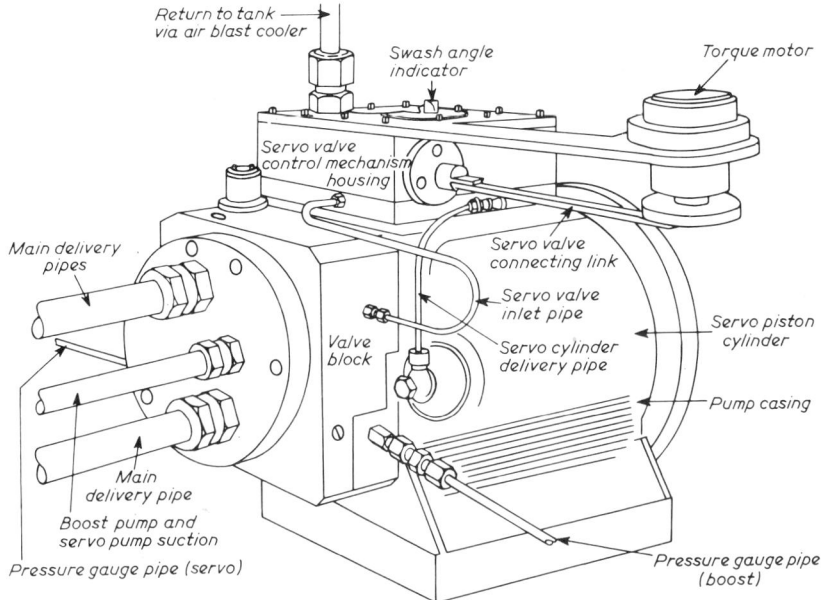

Return to tank
via air blast cooler

Swash angle
indicator

Torque motor

Servo valve
control mechanism
housing

Main delivery
pipes

Servo valve
connecting link

Servo valve
inlet pipe

Servo piston
cylinder

Valve
block

Servo cylinder
delivery pipe

Main
delivery pipe

Pump casing

Boost pump and
servo pump suction

Pressure gauge pipe (servo)

Pressure gauge pipe
(boost)

FIG. 24.—*Hastie high pressure swashplate pump.*

At the cut off position, the open centre of the valve bypasses the oil from the pump back to the suction side, while the bars of the control valve seal the ports to the main cylinders, locking the oil in the cylinders and holding the rudder firm.

When the helm is operated, the valve closes the bypass and simultaneously communicates the delivery of oil to one cylinder while opening the other cylinder to the suction side of the pump. The consequent transfer of oil moves the rudder actuator and hence the tiller and rudder. The movement of the tiller hunts the control valve back to the cut off position.

In some cases the control valve is operated by a solenoid controlled pilot valve similar to that illustrated in Fig. 8. Instead of being hand operated at the bridge, the switch is connected to the central point of the floating lever so that hunting gear characteristics can be provided.

6.7.2. Non-follow Up Steering—Fig. 2(e)

Two ways in which the output of a fixed delivery pump is controlled by a solenoids operated control valve to provide non-follow up steering are described in Section 2.6.

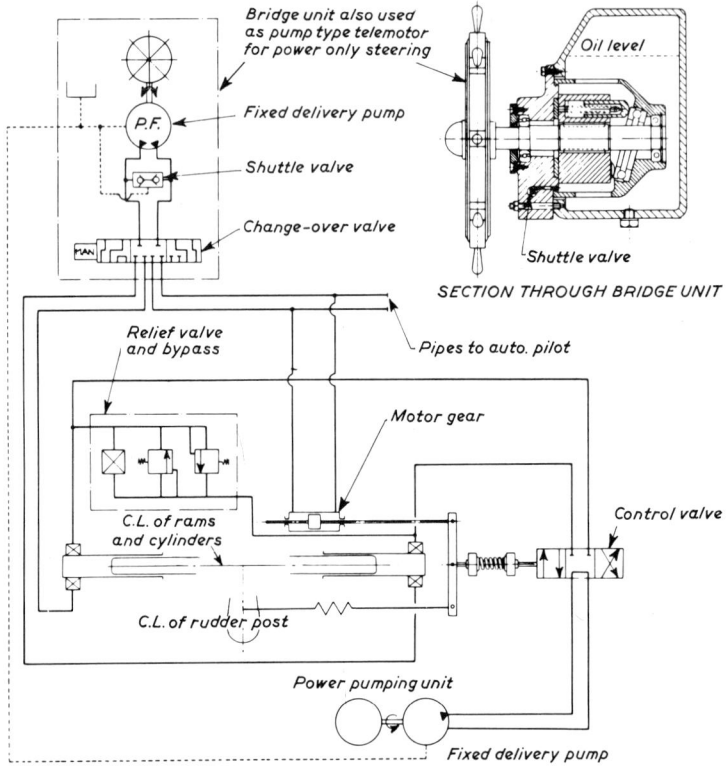

Fig. 25.—*Hand and power steering (hydraulic follow up control).*

6.8. Rudder Actuators

6.8.1. Mechanisms

The different mechanisms by means of which hydraulic power can be converted into torque at the rudder stock may be summarized as follows:

- a) Two or four ram gears incorporating the Rapson Slide acting on (i) round arm tiller (ii) fork tiller;
- b) One, two or four oscillating cylinders with single or double acting pistons driving crossheads or tillers;
- c) Two or four ram gears connected to crosshead by links;
- d) Single or duplicated rotary vane gears;
- e) Rotary piston operating direct onto the tiller.

6.8.2. Rapson Slide Actuators

Steering gears using the Rapson Slide mechanism are the ones most commonly fitted for high duty installations and of the two types in use the

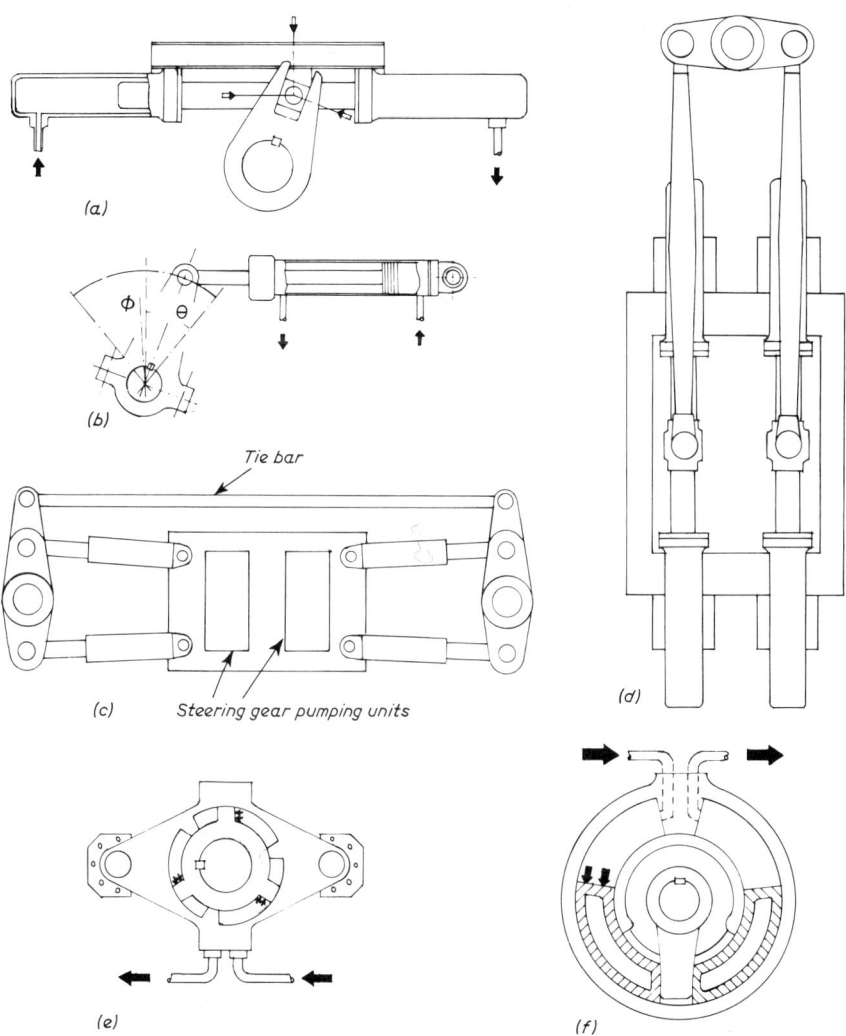

Fig. 26(a).—*Rapson slide mechanism with forked tiller.* (b) *Single oscillating cylinder steering gear.* (c) *Twin rudder installation using four oscillating cylinders.* (d) *Four cylinder link gear.* (e) *Rotary vane actuator.* (f) *Tenfjord rotary piston actuator.*

round arm tiller and crosshead arrangement is the most frequently found in service. Two cylinders in line or four cylinders for greater power and duplication can be used. Figure 26(a) shows a simple two ram Rapson Slide gear having a fork tiller and Fig. 27 a modern high pressure four ram Rapson Slide gear. This latter figure shows how the rams of each pair are coupled

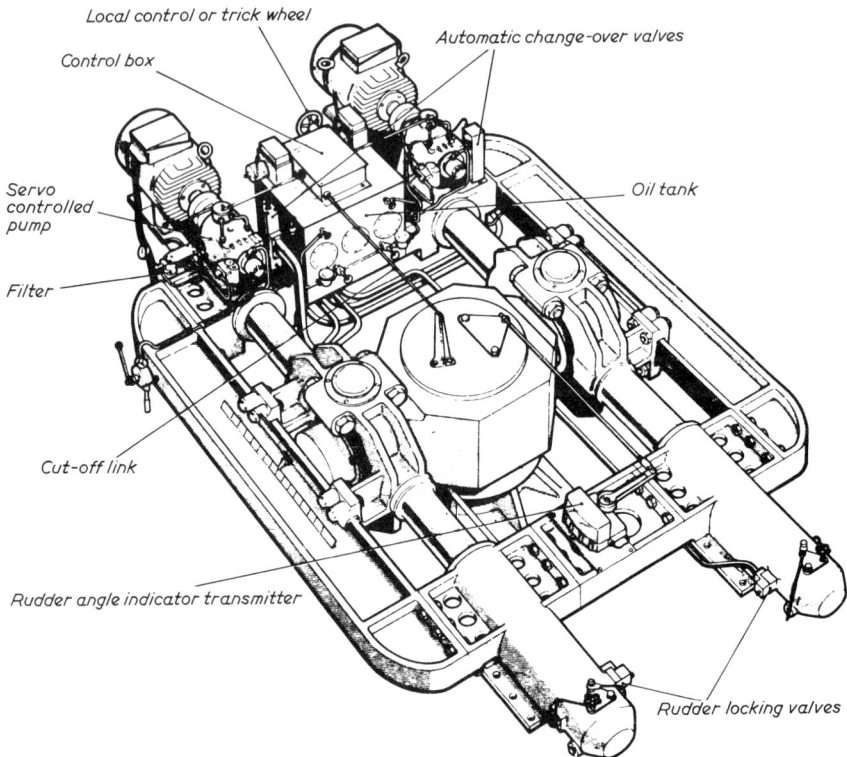

Local control or trick wheel

Control box

Automatic change-over valves

Servo controlled pump

Oil tank

Filter

Cut-off link

Rudder angle indicator transmitter

Rudder locking valves

FIG. 27.—*Brown Bros. four ram Rapson Slide steering gear with round arm tiller.*

together to form a double bearing in which the trunnion arms of a centre crosshead are mounted. The crosshead is free to slide along the circular arm of the tiller so that the straight line effort of the rams is applied to the angularly moving tiller.

In the case of the forked tiller design, the thrust from the rams is transmitted to the tiller through swivel blocks. One advantage of this arrangement is that the overall length of pairs of rams is reduced compared to the round arm tiller design and this can be an important consideration in some cases. A disadvantage is that whereas any slight misalignment in the case of the round arm tiller is not vitally important, it could lead to uneven loading of the swivel blocks in the forked tiller design and it is essential that the line of the rams be exactly at right angles to the rudder stock centre line if this is to be avoided.

With the Rapson Slide the torque reaction from the rudder is taken on the tiller by a force which is balanced by an equal and opposite force, having two components one of which is produced by the ram and acts in the line of

the ram, whilst the other is at right angles to the line of the ram and is produced by the guide reaction. These forces are shown on Fig. 26(a). Where
guides are not fitted as is sometimes the case with smaller steering gears then
the guide reaction force must be carried by bearings or the glands of the
cylinders.

With the rudder amidships, the torque T applied to the rudder stock
by the steering gear will be

$$T = p.a.n.r$$

where p = pressure
a = area of actuator
n = number of actuators
r = tiller radius

and at any rudder angle θ the torque applied will be

$$T = \frac{pa}{\cos\theta} \times \frac{r}{\cos\theta} \times n$$

$$= p.a.n.r.\frac{1}{\cos^2\theta}$$

and the Mechanical Advantage is

$$\frac{1}{\cos^2\theta}$$

which, neglecting friction is 1·49 at the rudder "hard over" angle of 35°.

6.8.3. Oscillating cylinders

The use of oscillating cylinders or pinned actuators—as they are commonly termed—has developed in recent years as these have become so
universally used in other branches of engineering. They can be used as single
cylinder units for hand only steering, single or two cylinder units for hand
and power steering, while four double acting cylinders can cope with the
larger torque demands. These units are double acting because pistons work
in the cylinders and pressure can be applied to either side as compared with
ram gears which are single acting.

Figure 26(b) shows a simple single pinned actuator arrangement and
Fig. 26(c) a four cylinder design for operating twin rudders.

In these cases, the torque T applied to the rudder stock varies with the
rudder deflexion angle and on the location of the actuator. In general, the
torque developed will be less at the maximum rudder angle than the maximum possible from the actuator.

Maximum torque from actuator $= p.a.n.r.$

Torque at $35° = p.a.n.r. \cos(35 \pm \phi)$
where ϕ = angle traced out by actuator
between $\theta = 0$ and $\theta = 35°$.
Mechanical Advantage at $35° = \cos 35° = 0.82$.

6.8.4. Rams connected to Crosshead by Links

Steering gears of this type—see Fig. 26(d)—are used if the athwartship space is very limited, or the head room at the rudder head is restricted, as for example in the case of a vehicle ferry or a whale factory ship having a slip way aft. The design enables the steering gear to be moved forward where there is reasonable head room for access.

As in the case of the oscillating cylinder design the Mechanical Advantage of the Rapson Slide gear is lost and the torque output of the gear is at a minimum at hard over when the torque demand created by the rudder hydrodynamic forces is at a maximum.

6.8.5. Rotary Vane Gears

These consist of two elements, a cylindrical static casing usually with three internal vanes and a rotor keyed to and concentric with the rudder stock which has matching vanes. The edges of the vanes are provided with seals, which are elastically loaded so as to ensure that contact with the mating surfaces is maintained in order to hold the hydraulic pressure. The vanes thus form the boundaries of compartments between the stator and the rotor as shown in Fig. 26(e). These compartments are alternately connected to the suction and delivery from the hydraulic pump so that low and high pressure compartments are created which produce the rudder actuating torque. Because the distribution of the pressure compartments is balanced around the rudder stock, only pure torque is transmitted to the stock and no side loadings are imposed by the gear.

There are two main designs of rotary vane steering gear in general use today. One of these, shown in Fig. 28, has the stator firmly attached to the deck and the stator housing and cover are provided with suitable bearings to enable the unit to act as a combined rudder carrier and rudder stock bearing support.

In the case of the vane gear illustrated in Fig. 29 the stator is only anchored to the ship's structure to resist torque but is free to move vertically, a separate rudder head bearing and carrier being provided as with ram type steering gears.

Rotation of the stator is prevented by means of two anchor brackets and two anchor bolts. The anchor brackets are securely bolted to the shipbuilder's stools and vertical clearance is arranged between the inside of the Stator flanges and the top and bottom of the anchor brackets to allow for vertical movement of the rudder stock. This clearance varies with each size

FIG. 28.—*Duplicated Donkin rotary vane gears operating twin rudders.*

of rotary vane unit but is approximately 38 mm total and it is essential that the rudder carrier should be capable of restricting the vertical movements of the rudder stock to less than this amount. The Anchor pins are fitted with special bushes in halves, shaped externally in order to pre-load the synthetic rubber shock absorbers which are fitted between them and the anchor brackets. The maximum deflection of the shock absorbers under full load is approximately 1 mm.

In the case of rotary vane steering gears the Mechanical Advantage is unity at all angles and hence the torque is constant.

$$\text{Torque} = p.a.n.r.$$

where n = number of vanes.

6.8.6. Tenfjord Rotary Piston Gear Actuator—Figure 26(f)

This gear consists of a casing around the rudder stock which contains pistons of rectangular section sliding in annular compartments concentric with the rudder stock. The tiller projects into a gap between the cylinders, the piston ends abutting onto the tiller but not being attached to it so that axial movements of the rudder cannot be transmitted to the pistons. Steering gears of this type operate at hydraulic pressures up to 41 bar (600 lb/in^2) and are generally restricted to low power applications.

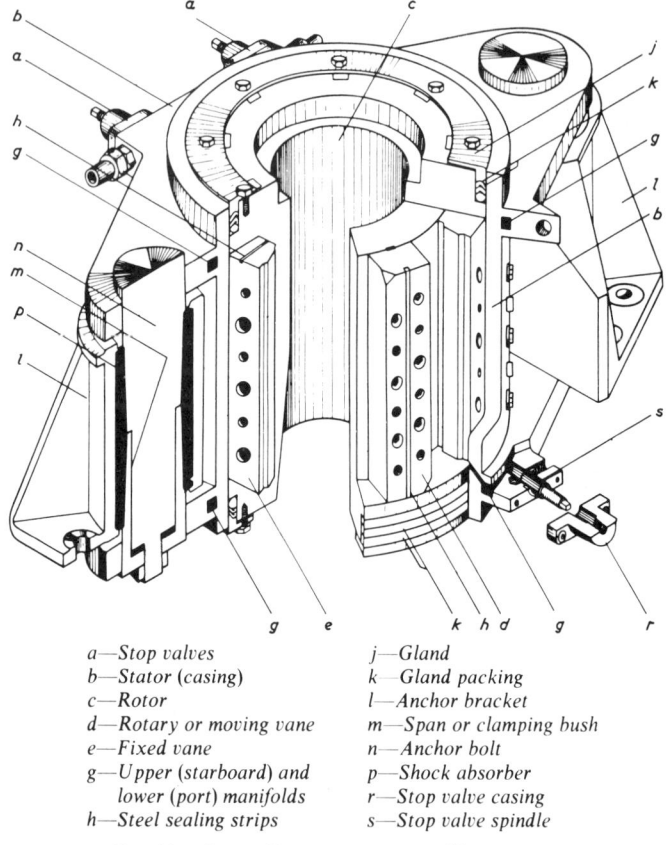

a—Stop valves
b—Stator (casing)
c—Rotor
d—Rotary or moving vane
e—Fixed vane
g—Upper (starboard) and
    lower (port) manifolds
h—Steel sealing strips

j—Gland
k—Gland packing
l—Anchor bracket
m—Span or clamping bush
n—Anchor bolt
p—Shock absorber
r—Stop valve casing
s—Stop valve spindle

FIG. 29.—*Brown Bros. rotary vane rudder actuator.*

As with the rotary vane steering gears the Mechanical Advantage is unity at all angles and hence the torque is constant.

$$\text{Torque} = p.a.n.r.$$

where n (in this case) is unity.

It can be seen that of all the different actuators in general use, the Rapson Slide gear gives the highest Mechanical Advantage. It is partly for this reason that it is widely used for steering gears since the torque demand from the steering gear increases and is a maximum at maximum rudder angle. Ram type steering gears are also well adapted to take advantage of the high pressures which are currently available (see Section 6.6) since ram diameters and casings are relatively small and leakage paths are small or non-existent.

6.9. GENERAL

6.9.1. Relief, Isolating and Bypass Valves

Hydraulic actuators are provided with relief and bypass valves between complementary pairs of cylinders or chambers of vane gears. The relief valves are set to lift at pressures above the normal maximum.

The bypass valves are normally closed but can be opened on a two cylinder gear to enable emergency steering to be used. On a four cylinder gear, one pair of cylinders can be bypassed while the other pair provides emergency steering at reduced torque.

Isolating valves are provided at each cylinder or rotary vane chamber which when closed will hold the rudder by trapping the oil in the chambers.

Isolating valves are also fitted to pumps so that a pump can be completely shut off from the circuit and removed for servicing while steering is continued with the other pump.

In the case of gears with duplicated variable stroke pumps, in order to be able to bring a standby unit quickly into operation, the pump stroke mechanisms are permanently coupled together and both pumps are left open to the hydraulic circuit. Thus it is only necessary to start up a motor for the stand by pump to be operative.

As a variable stroke pump can operate as a motor if pressure oil is applied to one side while it is on stroke, it is necessary to prevent windmilling or rotation of the pump which is on standby duty. Otherwise, the output of the operating pump instead of moving the steering gear would be used up in rotating the standby pump.

Figure 30 illustrates one method of preventing this, whereby a fixed ratchet is provided concentric with the pump driving shaft. Pawls which can engage this ratchet are carried in the drive coupling. When the pump is on standby the pawls engage with the ratchet and prevent rotation when oil on the delivery side of the operating pump is on pressure. In this condition the tendency to motor the stand-by pump will always be against its normal direction of rotation. As soon as the pump is started, rotation being in the opposite direction, the pawls dis-engage and by centrifugal action fling out against the inner flange of the coupling completely clear of the ratchet. When a pump is on standby and the rudder is being driven by water pressure in the direction in which it is being moved so as to generate pressure on what is normally the suction side of the operating pump, this will cause the standby pump to rotate in its normal running direction. This means that the pawls will disengage and the pump will be motored round, allowing the rudder to move more quickly to a new steering position than the single operating pump would allow.

A different method of protection involves the use of automatic change over valves as shown in Fig. 31. Each pumping unit is provided with a Servo pressure operated automatic change over valve which ensures that the pump can only be started in the unloaded condition and in addition prevents the standby pump from being motored by the pump in service. Functioning of

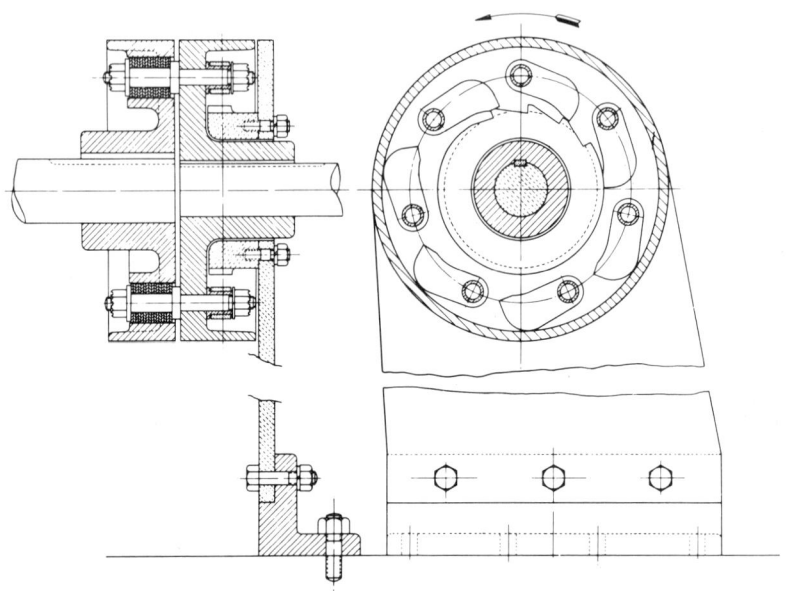

FIG. 30.—*Pawl mechanism for variable stroke pumps.*

the automatic change-over valve may be explained thus: when the associated pumping unit is stationary the valve is held in the bypass condition by the spring, thus isolating the pump from the main hydraulic system. By starting up the pump, pressure from the auxiliary unit associated with the pump builds up and overcomes the spring so as to move the valve into the "running" or "straight through" position, (i.e.) the bypass is closed and the pump is connected to the main hydraulic system. In the short time that elapses whilst the hydraulic pressure builds up sufficiently to operate the valve, the electric motor driving the pump attains its normal running speed so that the hydraulic load is effectively held off until the high starting current in the motor dies away. On stopping the motor, the spring returns the valve to the bypass condition.

The constant pressure line from the auxiliary pump on the other pump unit is connected to the spring end of the change over valve, but operates on a reduced area compared with the full area of the valve end, on which the pressure of the servo system of the associated pump operates. A "bleed" line is run from the spring chambers of each changeover valve to the tank to ensure that it can never be hydraulically locked by fluid leaking past the valve into the chamber.

No special provision against the motoring of a stand-by pump is required in the case of the variable stroke pump shown in Fig. 24 since control is effected solely by a slide valve. When on standby duty this valve

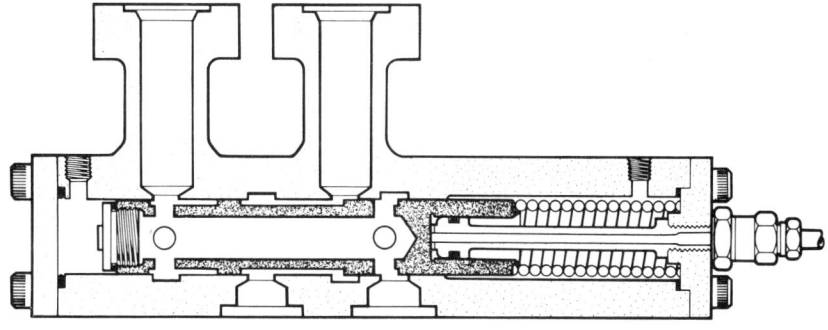

STRAIGHT THROUGH CONDITION

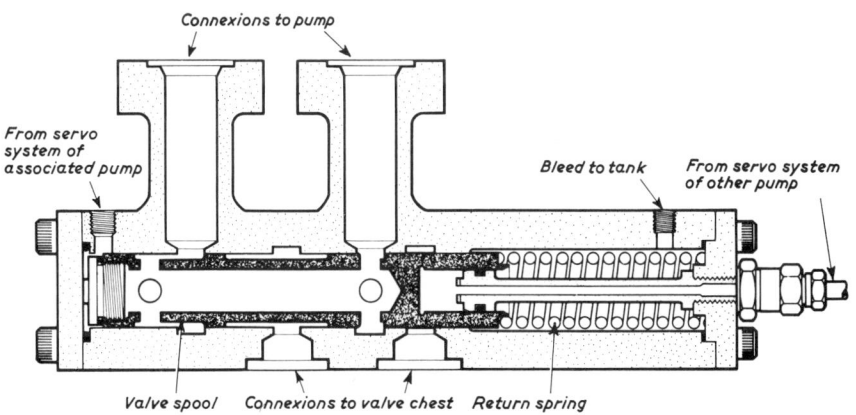

BYPASS CONDITION

Fig. 31.—*Brown Bros. automatic change over valve.*

is retained in the mid position so that the pump remains in the zero stroke condition and, hence, cannot be motored by the pump in service.

Where fixed delivery pumps are duplicated in supplying oil to a common hydraulically operated control valve, an automatic change-over valve can be fitted which will isolate the standby pump when it is at rest, but will connect it to the actuator when the pump is started up.

Pumps with solenoid operated valves are sealed from the actuator by the control valve in the manner indicated above unless a solenoid is energized. The electric circuit should therefore be arranged to isolate the solenoids when the pump is not in use.

6.9.2. Stops and Limit Switches

Stern post stops set an absolute limit to hardover movement of the rudder. Mechanical stops on the rudder actuator operate before the stern post stops are reached. These take the form of deck stops for a quadrant or tiller of a steam or direct electric steering gear and travel limits on a ram, rotary vane or piston gear. Stops on the bridge control are set to act before the mechanical stops on the actuator. If the local control stops are separate, they are set between the bridge control stops and actuator mechanical stops. If there is an automatic helmsman its power unit stops are set inside the manual control stops.

In the case of non-follow up or time dependent gears limit switches or valves are tripped by the actuator before it reaches its mechanical stops.

The other type of stops on the steering gear are those that check the maximum travel from each side of the cut off position of a steam valve, hydraulic valve, pump stroke or switch and are set to operate just before these various controls reach the limit of their travel so that no undue loads can be applied to these parts.

6.9.3. Drive Back

A drive back load caused by heavy seas striking the rudder can be sufficiently large to produce a pressure in the actuator in excess of the relief valve setting, in which case the actuator and rudder will move. If the steering gear is provided with hunting gear, it will move out of co-incidence with the bridge control so that as soon as the load is removed, the gear will automatically return to its original position. Non-follow up gears will require to be brought back to the original position by the helmsman who will be notified of the movement of the gear by the rudder indicator.

6.10. Hand and Power Hydraulic Steering Gears

On small ships such as coasters, tugs, trawlers and yachts it is frequently desirable to steer by hand and by power; for ordinary course keeping at sea, hand steering can be used, while in crowded waters or narrow channels where frequent rapid changes of helm are necessary, power steering can be resorted to. Bridge chain gears provided the only effective way of giving these facilities until the introduction of the hand and power hydraulic steering gear, which in addition to doing away with the chain transmission and all its problems, also provides a much more efficient transmission of hand steering than was possible with the old mechanical arrangement.

A fixed delivery rotary pump of the type described in Section 2.4 and Fig. 7 is driven by the steering wheel and connected direct to the main cylinders when hand steering.

There are different methods of controlling power steering, the main types being as follows:

   a) "Follow Up" steering, the handwheel being used for both power and hand steering, transmission being hydraulic throughout;

b) "Follow Up" steering, the telemotor receiver controlling a solenoid operated control valve;

c) "Non-follow Up" power steering controlled by right and left hand switch on bridge operating solenoid control valve.

6.10.1. "Follow Up" Steering with Hydraulic Transmission Throughout

The "Follow Up" power steering circuit is as shown in Fig. 25 and as described in Section 6.7.1.

If an automatic helmsman is fitted, its solenoid operated control valve can be connected direct to the telemotor receiver. The problem of maintaining the balance of the two sides which prevents this practice with a bypass type telemotor does not arise with the pump type telemotor, also the same charging oil is used throughout.

A changeover valve with three positions is provided on the steering console. In the "Hand" position, the bridge pump is connected direct to the rudder actuator, the telemotor receiver pipes are bypassed, while the control valve of the automatic helmsman seals off its connection to the receiver. The main control valve is held by a spring in the cut off position which seals the power pump from the actuator.

Thus, as the rudder moves in response to the hand steering of the helmsman, a spring holds the control valve and centre point of the floating lever still, but because the receiver is bypassed, the end of the floating lever to which it is connected moves freely as the other end of the floating lever is moved by the tiller.

With the change over valve in the "Gyro" position, the bridge unit pump is cut off and the gyro pump operates the telemotor receiver direct, while all the pipes from the bridge control are sealed at the change-over cock.

When the change over valve is in the "Power" position, the bridge unit pump is connected to the receiver, and the hand gear pipes are sealed, while the gyro power unit is sealed off by its solenoid operated control valve. Manual control of power steering from the bridge can then be carried out.

6.10.2. Svendborg Hand and Power Steering System

Another system which provides hand and power steering from the bridge in which the power control is hydraulic, and which has been fitted on many ships is illustrated in Fig. 32. The power pump is a radial variable stroke reversible pump with a double row of pistons.

When power steering, pump stroke is applied by oil from the hand-wheel pump acting on piston 6, displacing the pump carriage. This causes pistons 4 to pump oil back to the handwheel pump. When the handwheel is held, this return oil presses opposite piston 6 so as to hunt off the pump stroke, pistons 3 discharge oil to displace the locking valve in the base of the pump so as to connect the pump to the main actuator and move the rudder.

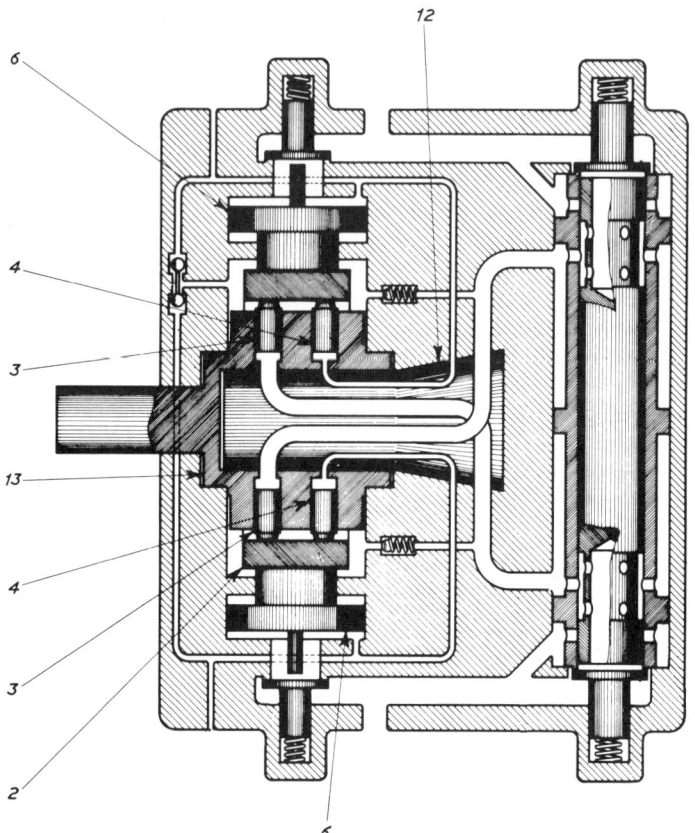

FIG. 32.—*Svendborg control system giving follow up steering.*

Should the power pump stop, changeover to hand steering occurs automatically, oil pressure from the handwheel pump lifts the non-return valve at one end of piston 6 and displaces the pump sliding carriage to lift the opposite non return valve, this connects the handwheel pump direct to the rudder actuator, maintaining control by direct hand steering.

6.10.3. "Non-Follow Up" Power Steering

This arrangement (Fig. 8) is the cheapest in conjunction with an automatic helmsman, because the manual power control from the bridge is provided by the automatic helmsman unit as described previously in Section 3.2. There is no need to duplicate the control circuit to meet Rule requirements because the hand steering from the bridge provides an acceptable alternative.

6.11. CHARGING

It is essential to use a grade of oil recommended by the steering gear manufacturer. In all cases a high quality hydraulic oil should be used containing inhibitors against oxidation, foaming, rust and wear and emulsification.

In order to keep the transmission load as low as possible when hand steering, hand power gears must have an oil of sufficiently low viscosity and low pour point, (e.g. No. 1 Redwood at 21°C (70°F) e.g. 125 to 250 at 29°C (−20°F).

The grade of oil for power only hydraulic steering gears is decided by what is the most suitable oil for the pumps fitted. The range is so great that it is not possible to be specific here, reference must be made to recommendations by the steering gear manufacturer.

Thus oils with No. 1 Redwood viscosities from 800 to 1500 at 21°C (70°F) are recommended for gears with Hele–Shaw pumps, while manufacturers' recommendations range from No. 1 Redwood viscosity at 21°C (70°F) of 150 to 800 for swashplate pumps. A similar wide range covers the various fixed delivery pumps used.

Absolute cleanliness is essential. Before charging, all pipes, cylinders, valves, tanks, etc. of the system should be thoroughly cleaned and inspected. Clean linen cloths should be used, never waste. Before any plugs or fittings are unscrewed, the area around, and any containers or strainers used should be thoroughly cleaned. Oil poured into any part of the system should be put in through filters.

Procedure
1) Remove coupling bolts between motors and pumps, start motors to check that rotation is correct; replace coupling bolts.
2) Fill cylinders of ram gears or vane gears; replace filling plugs. Close air plugs.
3) Fill supply tank below Hele–Shaw pumps or overhead supply tanks of swashplate and fixed delivery pumps.
4) Open cylinder bypass valves, and make sure valves from supply tanks are open. Open air valves on top of swashplate and fixed delivery pumps until oil free of air comes out; close air valves, replenish supply tank.
5) Put stroke on variable stroke pumps or open control valve using local control.
6) Turn pump by hand releasing air at appropriate cylinder. Repeat other side.
7) Start up motor.
8) Move local control side to side.
9) Close bypass valve checking that when actuator moves pump stroke or control valve is hunted off, and that movement is in direction of helm order.

TABLE IV—FAULTS, CAUSES AND REMEDIES IN HYDRAULIC STEERING GEARS*

Fault	Cause	Remedy
1. Too much steering wheel movement before engine moves.	a) Slogger in control and hunting gear mechanism.	Repair and replace pins and bushes.
	b) Excessive lap on control valve.	Correct.
	c) Air in system.	Blow off. Make sure replenishment tanks charged and that they are open to system. Check that joints and gland packing are air-tight. If auxiliary pump fitted, check that it is functioning correctly. Check that suction valves in order. It is particularly important to see that air is not drawn in at auxiliary pump and suction valves.
2. Rudder movement too slow.	a) Bypass valve not shut tight.	Check and make sure valve and seat not damaged. Repair.
	b) Relief valve leaking.	Check that valve and seat not damaged, and spring not broken. Check setting.
	c) Stroke stops on variable stroke pumps set in.	Check setting.
	d) Pump drive below speed.	Check speed.
	e) Abnormal internal leak in pump.	Check output at relief valve setting. If inadequate check pistons, cylinders and valve for scoring and wear. Repair and renew as necessary.
	f) Leak across worn control valve.	Renew.
	g) Abnormal load on actuator due to seizure or damage in rudder or rudder post.	Check pressure to move rudder in still water—should not exceed 14 bar (200 lb/in^2).
	h) If movement normal in local control but slow in manual control of automatic helmsman unit.	Check speed of control movement.

Symptom	Cause	Remedy
3. Rudder and gear "hunt" when helm still at midships.	Badly worn bearings.	Causes slogger of rudder stock, movement of which is sufficient to move hunting gear feed back far enough to put stroke on pump or open control valve to gear. Repair bearing.
4. Rudder and gear "hunt" when helm still and away from midships.	Leak from one side of system to other due to leak across bypass valve or relief valve—or internal leak in pump as in 2e) or across control valve 2f).	See 2a) and b). If sufficiently severe such leaks would allow actuator to be pushed back towards midship by pressure of the water on the rudder until the hunting gear moves the control so as to drive the gear back to original position. Locate leak and repair.
5. Non-follow up gear will not hold rudder over.	As in 4 above, but no hunting gear to restore angle.	Locate and repair.
6. Helm, tiller, rudder and rudder indicator not simultaneously midships.	a) Rudder indicator needs adjustment.	a) Adjust if tiller is midships and indicator is not.
	b) Check that control correctly connected to helm actuator.	b) See Table 1—8b).
	c) Stock twisted if helm actuator and tiller midships and rudder not.	c) Adjust so that rudder is midships when helm midships temporarily. Repair stock.
7. Control stiff to operate but free if disconnected from gear (see 6b).	Binding in hunting gear, pump stroke mechanisms or control valve.	Examine, free and lubricate.
8. Noise and vibration from pump.	a) Excessive amount of air in system.	a) See 1c).
	b) Misalignment of coupling between pump and motor.	b) Check and correct.
	c) Mechanical fault in pump.	c) Examine for ball or roller bearing failure. (Valves are provided so that steering can be continued with other pump while pump under examination is shut off system.)

* Detailed cases in individual systems cannot be given here; the above is a general guide only.

10) Check setting of hardover stops.
11) Work gear side to side blowing off air always ensuring that valve is on cylinder into which oil is being pumped.
12) Release air accumulating in swashplate and fixed delivery pumps.
13) Connect Bridge Control check direction and hardover stops.

7. AUXILIARY MEANS OF STEERING

7.1. RULES

The Rules require that all ships are provided with an efficient main and auxiliary steering gear; see Section 1.

7.2. STEAM STEERING GEAR

In the case of steam steering gears the requirement for power operated auxiliary steering is usually met by providing shackles on the tiller or, as in Fig. 14, on the quadrant so that ropes can be led to some other deck auxiliary such as the capstan or a winch.

7.2.1. Wilson–Pirrie Gears

These gears are mounted on double bedplates as shown earlier in Fig. 14. The top bedplate (8) in Fig. 14 is bolted to the lower fixed bedplate (7) through slotted holes which allow the engine to be drawn back until pinion (5) is disengaged from quadrant (2). The quadrant and rudder are held stationary whilst the changeover is being made by screwing the friction brake (12) against quadrant (11).

To cover the case of a buffer spring (3) breaking, a jaw (15) is formed on the end of the tiller sufficiently wide to allow full spring movement of a lug (16) which is cast on the quadrant. Screws (17) in the jaws can be tightened up to hold the quadrant and tiller together.

In the event of damage to the tiller, a key can be inserted into keyway (4) in the quadrant boss and rudder stock, thus cutting out the tiller.

7.3. HYDRAULIC STEERING GEARS

With one pump, these can be accepted provided suitable provision is made in the form of an extension tiller on the tiller boss to which a deck auxiliary can be connected with ropes and shackles as in Section 7.2. In any such case the single pump would be required to put the gear from hard over to hard over in the time required by the Rules, (see Section 2).

In cargo ships, a two ram hydraulic gear with duplicated pumping units satisfies the requirement provided there is suitable duplication of power supply, although in the larger vessels it is generally the case that a four ram hydraulic gear is fitted.

In the case of passenger ships, more complete duplication is generally required, such as is provided by a four ram gear with duplicated pumping units.

7.4. Hand Operated Gears

In those cases where hand operated auxiliary steering is permitted by the Rules, a number of different alternatives can be employed. With chain operated steering gears, a right- and left-hand screw gear was often fitted. This device, which was patented in 1853 by John Hastie, provided for the first time a self-holding steering gear which resisted the kick-back effect of heavy seas on the rudder. Whilst this gear was perfectly satisfactory for small rudders, its lack of cushioning or slip under severe conditions led to its being superseded by gears incorporating worm and wormwheel drives, which were suitably protected against severe loading by the inclusion of a friction clutch between the wormwheel and the driving shaft.

7.5. Hand and Power Steering from the Bridge

Acceptable as alternative means of steering, provided the pipes used for the two different methods of control are separate and can be isolated from the system (Fig. 25).

In the case of hydraulic steering gears with power steering only from the bridge, a hand pumping unit placed aft with separate pipe leads to the cylinders is acceptable. This can take the form either of a handwheel operated pump, similar to the bridge unit pump previously described, or a ram pump with a change over valve, so that discharge and suction sides of the pump can be connected to the main cylinders according to which way it is desired to move the rudder.

8. SPECIAL STEERING DEVICES

8.1. The Kort Nozzle

Originally designed to reduce erosion of canal banks by the wash of tugs, the nozzle has proved itself also able to increase thrust without increase of applied power.

The nozzle consists of a ring of aerofoil section which forms a nozzle surrounding the propeller (Fig. 33). The suction action of the propeller causes an acceleration of flow in the mouth of the nozzle and hence a drop of pressure in this region. Since the pressure on the outer part of the nozzle remains relatively unchanged, there is a resulting differential in pressure, which acting on the projected annulus of the nozzle, gives the additional forward thrust. This additional thrust is transmitted direct from the Kort nozzle to the hull via the nozzle supports, so that no additional thrust loading is imposed on the propeller shaft thrust block.

There are two types of Kort Nozzles. The fixed type has a conventional rudder behind it, whereas with the swivelling rudder type, the whole assembly is supported by a carrier attached to the rudder stock and actuated by the steering gear.

In the case of nozzle rudders, when helm is applied, the increased thrust has an athwartship component which has a powerful steering effect, so that hardover angles of 25° (or 30° in special cases) are sufficient to provide effective steering ahead during a crash stop and, provided the hull is a reasonable design, astern.

This device is especially valuable for tugs, trawlers, special vessels and, more recently, VLCC, which are required to manoeuvre well, particularly at slow speeds, and have the best propulsive efficiency. Bollard pull gains between 30 and 50 per cent, equivalent to re-engining with up to $1\frac{3}{4}$ times the original power, have been obtained in tugs and trawlers and in VLCC gains in propulsive efficiency between 6 and 13 per cent can be expected.

The normal methods of calculating rudder torques cannot be applied to nozzle rudders, the manufacturers of which specify the torque which the steering gear has to produce from their experience of the rudders in service. To the figure they provide, steering gear and bearing friction must be added and provision should also be made for momentary peak torques of up to about 40 per cent more than the stated torque. The maximum steering effort is required to return the rudder towards midships and not to move the rudder

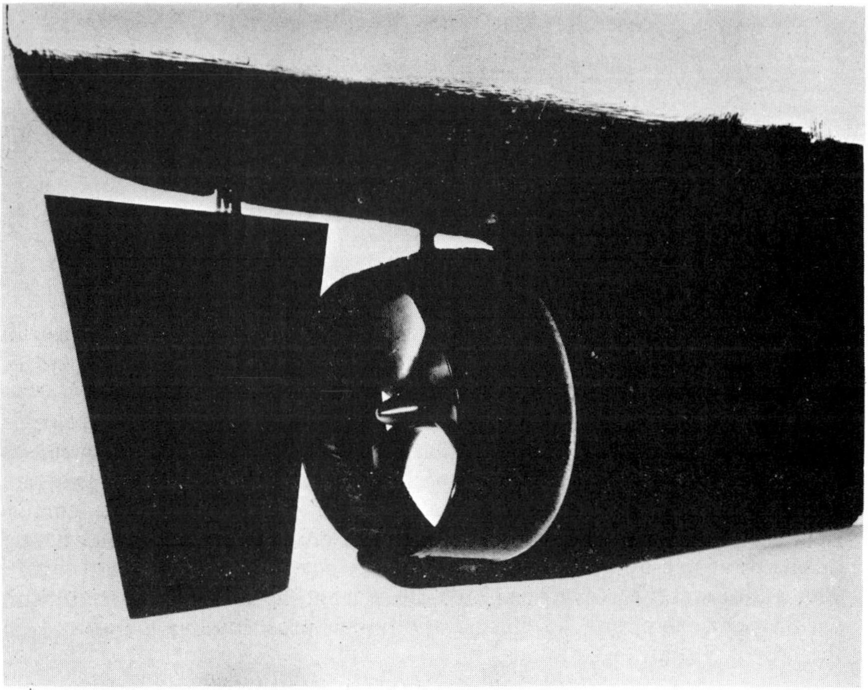

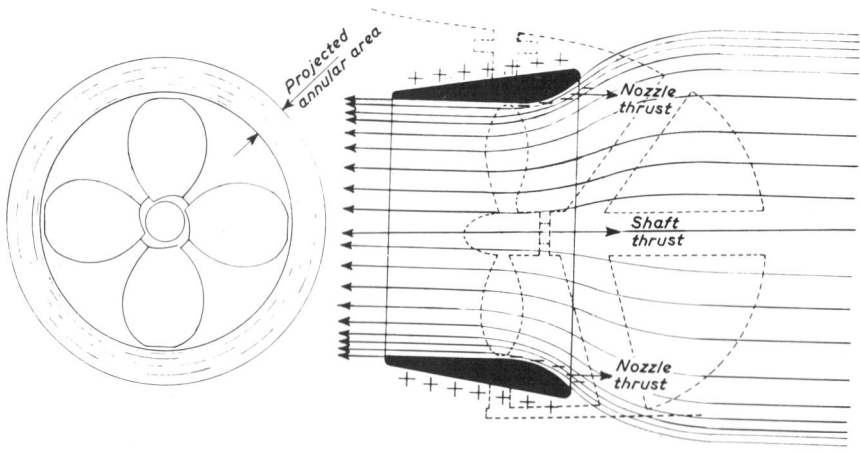

FIG. 33.—*Kort Nozzle.*

over from amidships. Thus, the steering gear must be designed to keep control of the rudder under these conditions.

8.2. PLEUGER RUDDER

A normal rudder can only be effective when the ship is moving, and the torque it can exert varies with the square of the speed, so that at very low speeds it can be very ineffective. A Pleuger Rudder (Fig. 34) incorporates a submersible electrically driven propeller which can be run when the main propulsion is at rest. Thus, that at very slow speeds or even when the ship is at rest, it can be manoeuvred by putting the rudder over and running the propeller in the rudder. In order to achieve the maximum effect and be able to turn the ship without any forward movement, this rudder can be put over to an angle of 90°. Owing to the large rudder angle it is not possible to use the conventional floating lever hunting gear for the steering gear, and a special cam operated hunting gear has to be employed. For normal course keeping with the ship proceeding at normal speeds, the angle of steering is limited to the conventional 35°, and a warning signal indicates when this angle is exceeded. When the ship is at rest, the rudder can be moved right over to the full angle and full manoeuvrability achieved.

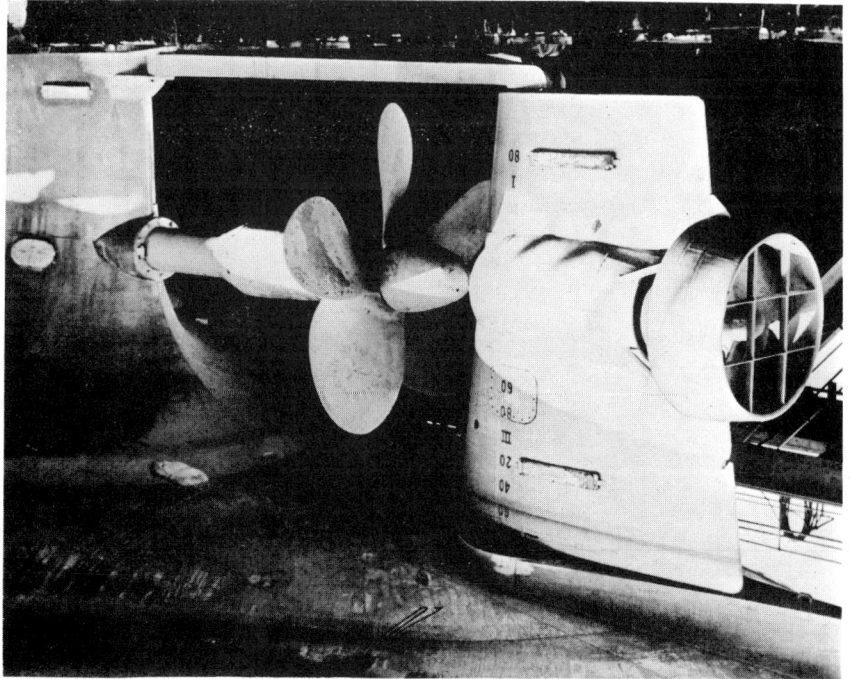

FIG. 34.—*Pleuger rudder.*

8.3. The Voith Schneider Propeller

This propeller consists of a series of blades of aerofoil section which project vertically downwards from the ship's hull and rotate about a vertical axis.

The blades are mounted on axes on a circle around the central axis and are linked together with a mechanism which can cause them to oscillate so as to provide thrust in any direction. The amount of thrust can be varied by varying the degree of oscillation, thus with the blade assembly rotating in the same direction, manipulation of the blades can give ahead or astern thrust, or port and starboard thrust without an ahead or astern thrust component, or any angle of port or starboard thrust with ahead or astern thrust.

Figure 35 shows the cycloidal motion of the blades which can be made to produce thrust in any direction round the circle of rotation. This means that the propeller in addition to providing the main drive for a ship provides full manoeuvrability without the need to provide a rudder and steering gear. This unusual degree of control is of particular value for special craft or floating equipment such as floating cranes or drilling ships which must be kept in position.

The location of the propeller depends upon the particular application and it can be placed where the maximum desired effect can be achieved.

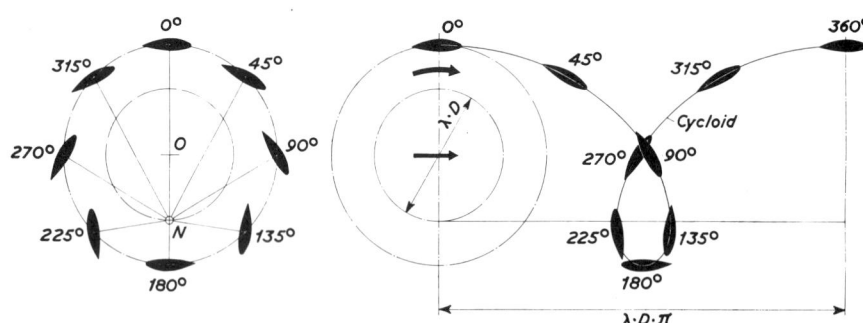

FIG. 35.—*Cycloidal path of a Voith Schneider propeller.*

8.4. Manoeuvrability and Stopping

The problem of improving the manoeuvrability and braking of ships is of increasing importance as they increase in size. One device which is being tried out to improve stopping power is to arrange the control of twin rudders so that they move outboard simultaneously. This involves two separate steering gears, one for each rudder, the movement of which must be synchronized for normal steering.

8.5. ROTATING CYLINDER RUDDERS

This is a device to make a ship equally manoeuvrable at all speeds and was developed in the U.K. by the Ship Division of the National Physical Laboratory (N.P.L.). Its principal of operation is shown in Fig. 36.

A normal rudder is effective up to angles of about 35°, after which the flow over the rudder stalls in a manner similar to that over an aeroplane wing at high angles of incidence. There are various methods of preventing this from occurring and they all involve feeding energy into the stream of fluid adjacent to the rudder or aerofoil surface. This is called *boundary layer control*. One such method is to rotate a cylinder at the leading edge of the section at such a speed that the rudder can be put over to 90° without stall, and this is the basic principle of operation of the rotating cylinder rudder. It is, of course, necessary to reverse the direction of rotation of the cylinder depending on whether the rudder is put to port or starboard, and such a system can be fitted to almost any type of rudder, balanced or unbalanced.

The major advantage of putting a rudder over to such a high angle is that the flow from the main engines may be deflected through a much larger

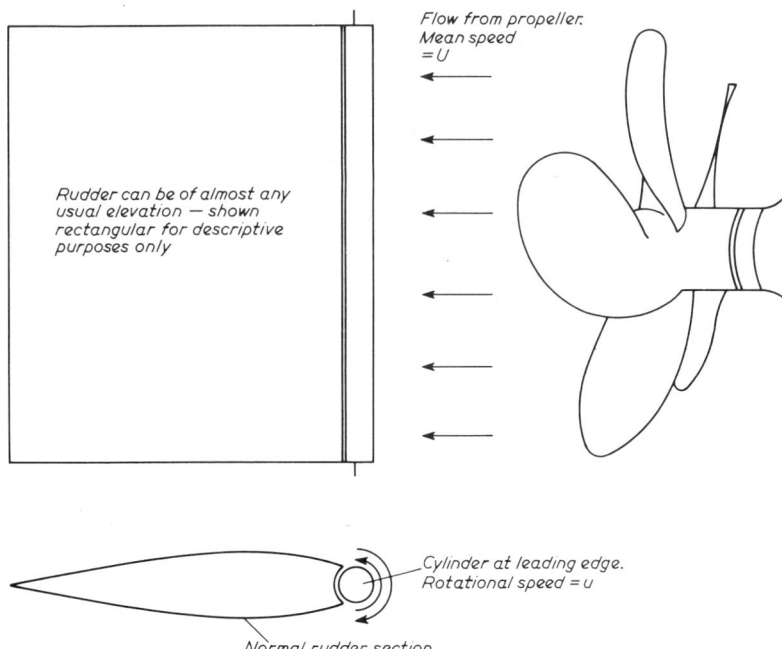

FIG. 36.—*Principal parameters of rotating cylinder rudder (this may be used with balanced or unbalanced rudders, u/U = constant).*

angle than with a conventional rudder, and static side thrusts of over 50 per cent of the bollard pull have been measured. Another main advantage is that its effect is independent of forward speed and it works as effectively at zero as at full speed.

8.6. Jet Flap Rudder

Another device which is being investigated at the N.P.L. is the jet flap rudder. In the trailing edge of an otherwise conventional rudder, a fluidic switch is fitted, which can direct a jet of water to port or starboard (Fig. 37). The water is pumped into the hollow rudder through a hollow rudder stock.

Considerable increase in manoeuvrability is claimed, especially at low speeds. There are of course other devices such as bow thrusters, but this Part is only concerned with steering gears operating rudders.

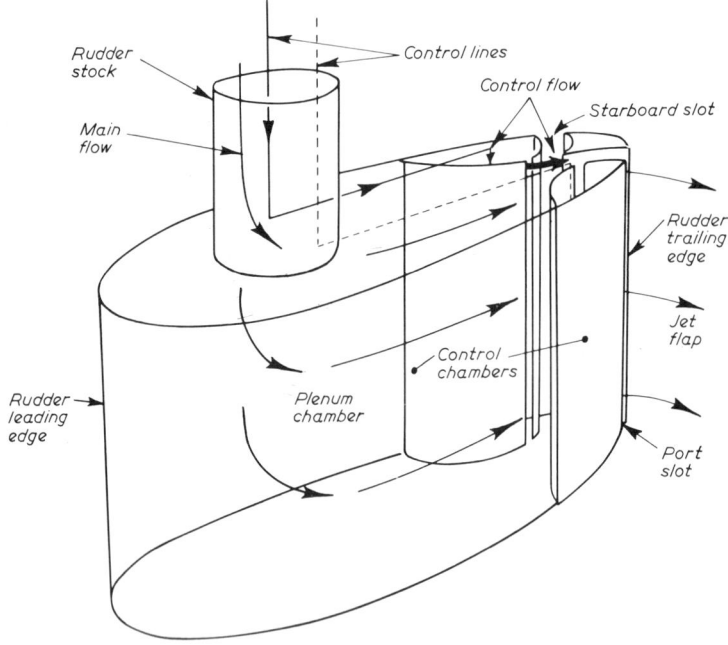

Fig. 37.—Jet flap rudder, showing fluidic switch.